THE ART OF FOOD AND BEVERAGE FESTIVAL PROMOTIONS

GUIDE FOR FOOD & BEVERAGE PROFESSIONALS

DR GAJANAN SHIRKE

Made with ♥ on the Notion Press Platform
www.notionpress.com

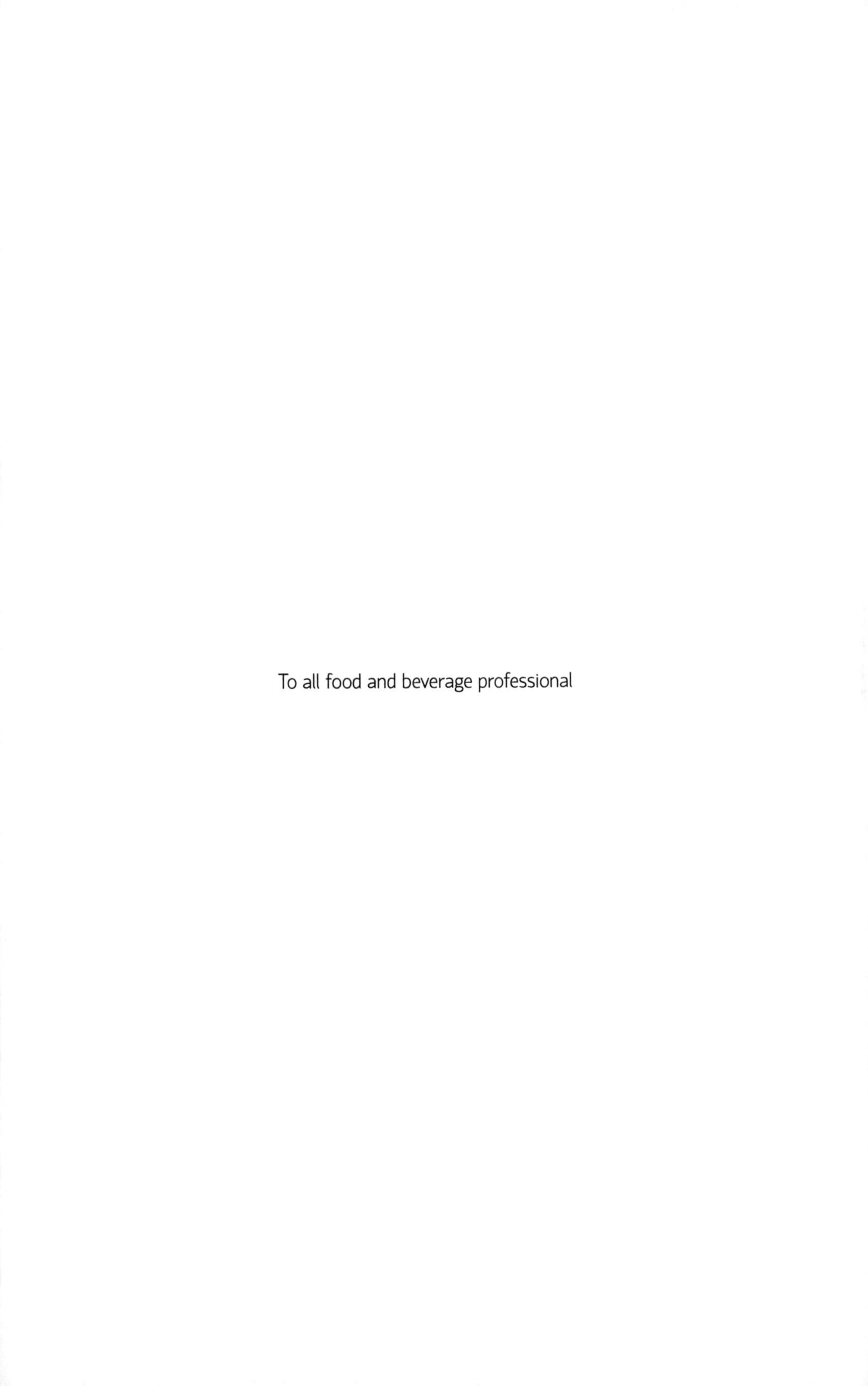

To all food and beverage professional

Contents

Preface

This book is meant for different festival and celebrations. The author has covered varies cuisines available in the market today without compromising on the final result. The book gives a beautiful description of some well-known global cuisines and festivals.

Acknowledgements

Acknowledgements

I would like to express a special debt of gratitude to my wife Rajeshree and my two daughters Rupeshi & Kavya, my teammates and superior leaders who encourages me to write.

Index

About Author

About the Author

Dr Gajanan Shirke, a hotel consultant, has years of extensive experience in the hospitality industry. His thirst for learning and aspiration to become a multi-faceted expert in the hotel industry helped him rise from employment to becoming an independent professional in the hospitality sector. Since his last assignment as General Manager at Kamat Hotels, he has become a renowned hotel consultant with a proven track record of developing, training and growing some of the best-known hotels, restaurants and fast-food joints in the Indian market. He was appointed as an expert consultant for The Eighth meeting of the Board of Studies for Hotel Management & Catering Technology. He is a visiting faculty at various Hotel Management Colleges and has trained over a thousand hospitality professionals. He has completed numerous pre and post opening hotel consultancies in India and overseas.

In order to spread his extensive knowledge to aspiring hotel professionals, Gajanan has penned a large number of books spanning different segments of the hospitality industry. Starting from his first book 'Bar Management and Operations' published in 2010, he has written 51 books including Hospitality Management, Food and Beverage Management, Hotel Engineering Management, Front Office Management, Hotel Housekeeping Management, The Cookery Trilogy: Advance Cookery Theory, The Cookery Trilogy: Foundation of Cookery, The Cookery Trilogy: The Basic Cookery Book, Hotel Sales and Marketing, Hospitality Industry Accounting & Fundamentals, Customer Interaction Excellence in Hospitality, History of Indian Cuisine – Volume 1, History of Indian Cuisine – Volume 2, Hotel Owner's Manual, Hotel Security & Prevention, Training Manager's Manual, Exceptional Service In Hospitality Six Sigma Way, etc.

CHAPTER ONE

Importance of Food Festivals

Food festivals are all about celebrating and enjoying food and drinks, with the current rise in 'foodie culture' these events are gaining popularity. Additionally, it gives a good reason for people to socialise, enjoy and experience variety of gastronomic extravaganza by attending it. It also gives an excellent opportunity for hotel and restaurant teams to connect with their customers, to showcase their diversity, quality, and uniqueness in their food and beverage offerings. As a result of any successful business, a well-planned and well executed food festival helps in improving customer satisfaction, loyalty, brand value and can act as an additional revenue stream.

Food Festivals have become quite popular in the past few years in the country and have received pretty great footfall. With the fusion of Social Media and Food, the food festivals in India are trending these days and gaining popularity by the second and more and more people are looking to connect to these events in one way or the other. Food fests are the hot new trend across globe.

Food festivals are an excellent platform for the upcoming as well as the established restaurants to market their goods and display their best offerings to the enormous crowd. It is a great medium to conduct market research and tests for future ideas and dishes.

Exposure to Relevant Audience: Restaurant Food Fests cater to a huge crowd which can prove wonders for your restaurant. The footfall is huge. Not only you get a vast exposure; the prime audience is the Foodies of your city. Thus, if you make a great impression on the visitors at your stall at the festival, there is a high probability that they would come to your restaurant again.

Staying In Touch With Your Competitors: While gaining customers is one aspect of a Food Festival, it also allows you to peek through other restaurants' strategies. Moreover, connecting with other restaurateurs can help in stepping up in the industry. Food Festivals let you interact with a large number of restaurateurs and gain insights about their problems and strategies to overcome them. This aspect of food fests makes them so important for restaurateurs.

Customer Connect: Festivals are a sure shot way to make some followers. Talking and connecting to people, especially tourists, and foreigners is a great way to generate word of mouth marketing. No marketing strategy is better than word of mouth and Food Festivals can create loads for you. You can also collect customer feedback and gather some first-hand data for your CRM as well.

Initiating Boost: Food Festivals can prove to be a catalyst for new or upcoming restaurants. If you have just opened or are planning to open in the next few months, eyeballs at food festivals will get you a head start that simple marketing just cannot do. Being new or first-timer at a festival can come with a loss of money due to low sales or sacrificing sales at your restaurant to accommodate the crowd at the festival but Food Festivals surely benefit you in the long run.

Publicity: Participating in a food festival gives you the opportunity to link on the event's marketing strategies. Your restaurant's name is publicized by the festival's marketing team in the Press Releases, E-mail Newsletters, Online and Offline Marketing techniques, and other possible promotions. You can also work on your social media platforms like Instagram and Facebook. All of this happens without you having to invest too many PR resources of your own.

As a restaurateur, you have the opportunity to present to the customer your best dish at a decent price so that the customer can decide whether they would like to return to your restaurant or not. With thousands of people visiting food festivals, your restaurant can get the stage which is required to launch or re-launch it in the restaurant industry.

While there are a variety of festivals with different underlying themes, the provision of food is commonplace in most festivals. The festival which simply includes a food component, however, cannot be classified as a food festival. A food festival is a food featured festival that really highlights what regional/local specialty food is or a food-themed festival which has food-based or food-themed activities and programme. A food festival is where communities engage in the public celebration and promotion of local food. It is one way of engaging with the other, and experiencing local/regional food.

CHAPTER TWO

Making Food Festival Successful

Planning: You'll need to understand how to delight your attendees with impeccable dining and event experiences.

Your events objective should be crystal clear. Motivation behind this food festival must be shared with the team responsible for organising the event.

Your concept/theme, your story, your uniqueness, your projected footfall and your budget: You might have a great concept, but equally good story will be required to sell it to customers, with highlights of your uniqueness of the festival. For example, non-residence foot fall has increased.

Forcasting: Make the Profit and Loss analysis based on forecasted footfall, during the planning stage. While making your budget, be realistic and creative. Find out cost for various elements of the event; Entertainment, décor, branding, marketing, staffing, admin cost.

Your target audience: To decide, on what do you want in the event; live music, only food or beverages, cultural event, kids area or any other factor, firstly, you must be clear on who you will be targeting. Consider demographics, age, income levels, and current trends decide on your target market. Decision on your audience will help you to get better understanding of your theme.

Timing of the festival should be well-thought-out to attain success. Consider seasons of the year, summer, winter, public holidays, sporting event, religious festivals/holidays, school holidays.

in which Food & Beverage outlet it will be?: Depending on your planned theme, availability and area of the venue, your estimated footfall, entertainment space, ease of services, required bar area and budget will help you to make a right decision on the location. However, let's say you have one location only and that's you restaurant then décor it accordingly.

Marketing and PR: A good marketing and PR activity with solid, simple and valuable concept will make your event irresistible. Remember three things, Promote, Promote and Promote. Don't leave any opportunity to promote, begin with startling looking creative which goes well with the theme. Creative, should be simple with very few words. Advertise on both paid and free medium; social media, radio, outdoors, newspaper ads, videos, event pictures, blogs, whatsapp and press conference. You can also engage your audience online via contests. Appoint a person only for tele-calling marketing. Depending on the size of the event we get sponsored by food and beverage partners. Most importantly, if your budget allows, you must do the outdoor at a high footfall location of the city/locality. On the other hand, you might have lot of budget and you can hire an agency and use the entire medium for marketing and PR to ensure success of the event. Even so, don't forget to reach the right people at the right time.

- Media partners will help you reduce your need for advertising expenses.
- Incorporate festival into existing advertising, public relations, and marketing campaigns.
- The event brochure print production schedule will help drive festival planning deadlines.
- Create individual press releases on every production element for the festival.

Sponsorship Checklist:

- Research comparable events elsewhere and replicate their successes.
- Target sponsors to offer cash, goods and advertising value.
- Create a presenting sponsor category.
- Create major sponsorship categories (i.e., auto, financial, beverage, media, etc.).
- Create sponsor categories for each of the programming areas.
- Do not allow sponsors to roam on-site during the event.
- Identify sponsor requirements early such as electricity, water, etc., and notify the operations team to determine the best locations.

Execution: Appoint core team with clarity on accountability and responsibility to ensure success of this festival. Take all the required permissions, food safety or any other licenses to avoid likelihood of risk during this festival. Consistency in quality, while pursuing excellence in services will increase your word of mouth marketing. Key in execution, is to deliver on customer expectations and WOW them with Variety, Quality, Efficiency, and Excellence in services.

There are various themes and variety of food festival that can be planned and executed have covered few festivals in this book. However, to make any food festival successful you may have to follow a good strategy, with implementing these proven fundamental techniques you will be able to achieve growth in your business. These methods will not only improve forthcoming event by growing your footfall, improving your positioning in the market and ROI on food festivals, but also boost your future business prospects.

Prepare Entertainment Acts: Music can definitely be a good way to both enhance the atmosphere and attract more people. There are many acts to choose from, such as singers, dancers, bands, and different kinds of DJs playing different types of music. Make sure the performance will fit in with the vibe of the event. It would also be great to have some artists or face painters to entertain everyone. Try to set up a stage where people can watch the artists perform. Along the same lines, make sure you have some activities for kids, which would be fun for all the family.

Conduct Pre & Post-Event Surveys: Most event presenters prefer taking a survey post the event to find out how they can make their upcoming events better. We recommend you find out what your attendees are looking for in a food fest. You can use social media to conduct polls or use our survey feature to understand which cuisine they prefer and if there are any special dietary requirements. The best time to send out a survey is while they are booking their tickets. When you give them what they've been looking for, you set yourself apart from others for considering your attendee's views.

Create Memorable Moments: People take away a lot of memories from a food festival. It could be a food challenge your best friend suggested or eating chili at one of the food stalls. Give them an option to create more. Set up a photo booth with creative props and let your attendees remember you for the greatest food festival you've given them.

Offer Giveaways: As a goodwill gesture and your post-event protocols, you can thank your attendees by offering them souvenirs at your food fest. It can be in the form of personalized t-shirts, caps, drinking mugs or keychains with your food fest logo inscribed on them. Every time they use these items, it will take them down a delicious memory lane of stimulating their taste buds at your food fest. You may also get requests from them to make it an annual event if it's not one.

Pre Festival Checklist in Short

- Food wise, make sure you have a variety of different food options. Be sure to include food for people with food allergies, sensitivities and vegan/vegetarian options.
- If you're doing a theme make sure all your vendors know when you book them. Make sure you decorate according to theme as much as possible too.
- Now make sure you have a good location for your weather. If it's usually hot during the month that it's planned inside and out is a good option. If it's cold have it inside to be more comfortable.
- Get good chefs that have lots of experiences in cooking it possible chefs from other countries and continents.
- Lots of tables, benches and places to sit and chat. Include booster type chairs for younger kids. Don't forget napkins, straws, eating utensils and condiments some vendors may not supply them (be ready).
- Also I know its food, but have some form of entertainment. Music, someone to face paint, someone that can make balloon animals... these things are greatly appreciated by families (meaning it could lead them to stay longer). Some places do bounce houses, but that tends to require more work like needing someone to supervise.
- Make sure your location has great ample safe parking. Something that's accessible for everyone too. If it's a pay to park place talk to who you can about making sure the fee is reasonable
- Advertising is a must. Post info about it on every social media account possible. Have your friends and family do the same. If you have a local (or sort of local) radio station, tv station or newspaper pay for an ad to be in each. Pass out flyers at your local colleges, at your church, anywhere you can. Update your social media account and the event's with food pictures and ask all your vendors to do the same.

- Make sure you have reliable sponsors to help fund this event and spread the world.

CHAPTER THREE

Rangeelo Rajasthan

The Restaurant can be decorated in Rajasthani theme with a lot of activities like puppet shows, Pottery, Clay Art, Camel ride if possible, Photo Zone and Rajasthani Handicraft stalls. The puppet show can be attraction for the children alongside activities like pottery and clay art.

LAL MAAS (RED MEAT): Lal Maas contains spicy, mouth-watering tanginess of a traditional Rajasthani dish. A red, spicy meat curry that's straight out of the Royal kitchens of Rajasthan, this dish is prepared using prime portions of mutton that's marinated in curd and spices. The dish is a result of the extreme heat and limited access to water that was prevalent in this region. Its unique preparation style serves the purpose of preserving it well after it's cooked and the spices enhance ones immunity and metabolism. Lal Maas is best relished with rotis and rice.

SAFED MAAS (WHITE MEAT): A delicious lamb curry, Safed Maas literally translates into 'white meat' and is also known as the Royal Lamb Korma in most Rajasthan homes. The flavour of this dish lies in the perfect amalgamation of spices like onion, ginger, garlic, pepper and cardamom in its creamy white sauce curry.

DAL BATI CHURMA (LENTILS) : A meal in Rajasthan is incomplete without Dal Bati Churma, one of Rajasthan's most savoured, complete meals. The dish itself consists of Dal (Lentils), Baati (wheat bread balls) and Churma (Sweet powdered cereal), served with red chilli on top of it along with spicy garlic chutney with dry fruits like cashew, pistachio, almonds or raisins. The wheat bread ball is dipped in pure ghee and served hot in an earthen pot with a small vessel of Dal, red chilli, spicy garlic chutney.

GATTE KI KHICHDI: A favoured rice dish of Rajasthan, Gatte ki Khichdi or Ram Paulo as it is known, is a rice dish whose creation is credited to the scarcity of green leafy vegetables in this desert region. Gatte ki Khichdi is prepared with spices, green peas, boiled/fried besan dumplings and aromatic rice. These flavours blend into a mouth-watering, flavourful meal that is traditionally served with a chutney or curd on the side.

KACHORIS: A breakfast in Rajasthan can be accompanied by a delicious Kachori, but one can enjoy this sweet and spicy snack any time of the day. Kachoris have been an integral part to the Rajasthan cuisine for quite some time now. Two famous variations of this snack are; the Pyaj Kachori (Onion Kachori), which is filled with a spicy onion filling, and Mawa Kachoris, filled with the sweet scented blend of mawa (condensed sweet milk) and nuts.

SHAHI GATTE: Shahi Gatte (and sometime known as Govind Gatte), is deep fried besan (chickpea) dumpling that is stuffed with a generous amount of indigenous nuts. Usually made of curd, the gravy of this dish is thick, delicious and can be enjoyed with a portion of rice or hot rotis.

MACHALEE JAISAMANDI: This Rajasthani dish is a flavourful delight that gets your taste buds working overtime. A tender serving of fish is cut and marinated in a green chutney, then further cooked in a savoury, spicy gravy that contains ginger, garlic, coriander and mint leaves.The dish is enjoyed with a helpful serving of rice and garnished with mint leaves and ginger juliennes.

MIRCHI BADA: This popular spicy snack is enjoyed especially in in Jodhpur during monsoon. It is prepared by splitting a mirchi (green chilli) and stuffing it with spices, a layer of mashed potato and gram flour. The green chili is first fried with the potato and masala and then deep fried with the gram flour over it. Chowdhry and Surya Namkin's Mirchi bada, and the Raju Mirchi bada are a few variants of this dish that are local favourites.

GHEVAR: Ghevar is a very popular filigreed Rajasthani sweet and its roots can be traced back to Jaipur. It is traditionally associated with Teej and Rakshabandhan festival. Primarily made of all-purpose flour and soaked in sugar syrup, it is shaped like a disc. Ghevar exists in different versions such as plain, mawa and malai. Rajasthan has always been a haven for the adventurous foodie, and one must experience the journey of flavours of this royal state.

KER SANGRI: Unique to the arid land of Rajasthan, Ker Sangri is a delectable amalgamation of ker, a shrub berry and sangria, a bean of the Khejari tree. Cooked simply with ingredients such as red chillies, carom seeds and spices, this bean and berry vegetable is flavourful, tangy and delightful. It is considered to be one of Rajasthan's most authentic gourmet preparations and is a must at Marwari wedding celebrations.

Panchmel ki Sabzi: It is a very popular, healthy and delectable dish from Rajasthan that derives its name from the combination of five ingredients used to prepare it. This extremely luscious and dry vegetable dish is prepared out of five vegetables seasoned with a mix of aromatic spices and gets its tangy flavour from the use of dried mango powder called amchur. It is best savoured with roti/chapatti and rice.

Khichdi: Whenever we talk of Khichdi, we consider a wholesome and healthy meal made out of rice and different pulses. However, people of Rajasthan have some innovative and nutritious preparations of khichdi that are made using wheat, jowar and bajra in place of rice. Some of the popular ones are Gehun ki Bikaneri Khichdi made of wheat and moong dal that can be enjoyed with ghee, curd and mango pickle; and Bajra khichdi made of bajra (black millet) and yellow moong dal (split yellow gram) and served with either curd or raita.

Gatte ki sabzi: This is an easy to digest and popular curry of Rajasthan made of gram flour balls with the gravy being prepared of buttermilk and different spices. It can be relished with both roti and rice.

Shahi Gatte: Shahi Gatte or Govind Gatte, is a rich and popular dish which consists of a gravy with fried besan dumplings that are stuffed with nuts. It can be savoured both with roti and rice.

Rajasthani Kadhi: Unlike the kadhi preparations of many of the other states like Punjab and Maharashtra, the Rajasthani Kadhi does not contain pakoras or gram flour dumplings. It is a very quick and easy preparation that is made with spiced yogurt based gravy that is thickened with gram flour.

Alwar ka Mawa / Kalakand: It is a famous sweet dish that originated from Alwar, Rajasthan. Prepared by thickened and solidified milk, paneer, sugar and dry fruits, kalakand today finds place not only in various Indian festivals and occasions but also in most of the sweet shops across the nation.

Rabodi Ki Sabzi : Rabodi Ki Sabzi is one of the oldest traditional dishes from Rajasthan; and is made from buttermilk and makai.

Mohan Thaal: Mohan Thaal is basically gram flour (besan) fudge infused with cardamom flavour, and topped with sliced almonds and pistachios. With chewy texture and sweet grainy taste, when you're craving something a little sweet, this could be your dish. It is popular in both Rajasthan and Gujarat.

Aam ki Launji: An instant pickle made of raw mangoes, this is a sure heat beater. It is prepared with fennel and nigella with sweet and sour gravy texture. Soft mango chunks are added to enhance the flavour.

Kalmi Vada: A perfect tea-time snack, these deep fried gram dal crispies are best enjoyed with spicy green chutney. The chutney made of mint and chillies gives the perfect amount of heat.

Achari Arbi Recipe | Spicy Taro Root Curry: Achari Arbi is an Indian curry made by cooking Taro Root (Arbi) in a special gravy. The gravy is prepared using the same spices which are used for making Indian Pickles.

Jodhpuri Kabuli Recipe | Rajasthani Veg Biryani: Jodhpuri Kabuli is an exotic dish made with layers of rice & spiced vegetable gravy cooked in yogurt topped with croutons & dry fruits.

Besan Mirch Recipe | Rajasthani Besan Ki Mirchi Recipe: Besan Mirch is a spicy and appetizing Rajasthani speciality made by sautéing green chillies with spiced gram flour.

Mooli Ki Churi Recipe | Grated Radish & Tomato Salad: Mooli ki Churi is a quick variety of salad based on grated Mooli(Radish) that goes very well with Indian Food.

Tomato Garlic Chutney Recipe | Rajasthani Lahsun Ki Chutney: Tomato garlic chutney is a spicy & tangy chutney made from fresh raw garlic as the main ingredient along with onion, tomatoes & other spices.

Masala Bati Recipe | Potato Stuffed Masala Bati: Masala baati is a traditional deep fried or baked bread from Rajasthan made by stuffing dough with a spicy mixture of potatoes & peas.

Panchmel Dal Recipe | Rajasthani Pancharatna Dal: Panchmel Dal is a traditional Rajasthani dal made my mixing together five different types of lentils along with a spicy tempering.

Aloo Pyaz Ki Sabzi: A popular authentic Rajasthani aloo pyaz paneer ki sabji. Potatoes, small onions (shallots) and paneer cubes are deep fried and then served in spicy tomato onion gravy. It is generally served with bejad roti or tikkad.

Rajasthani bhindi fry : This is also called Rajasthani bhindi ki sabji sukhiwali. This dish is very crispy and tasty because of addition of besan. Besan renders a fantastic taste. It makes the bhindi sabji crispy. Rajasthani bhindi fry is perfect dish for lunch and dinners. It goes well with Mix Rajasthani Dal or Gatte ki Sabji. Hot missi roti with this sabji and pickle is an epic combination.

Jaisalmeri kala chana: is a hidden gem from Rajasthani cuisine Because of unavailability of vegetables through out the year, Rajasthani food uses gramflour (besan), dahi, buttermilk, and dry masalas like dry ginger, kachhri a lot. Jaisalmeri kala chana recipe is like Rajasthani besan kadhi with kale chana. There is no Onion n Garlic. This kadhi needs very little time to prepare once the kala chana are boiled. Black chickpeas in yogurt curry tastes awesome with paratha or boiled rice.

Hare tomato aur moong vadi ki subzi : It is a tasty Rajasthani cuisine recipe that can be a refreshing change from everyday food. Made from delicious Moong dal ki vadi, green tomatoes, fresh spices, mustard oil, and tangy lemon, it is a healthy and delicious recipe that is easy to prepare at home.

Kaachar Batak: It is one of the traditional recipes of Marwari cuisine, where duck breast is traditionally tenderised with baby melons and cooked with red chillies, garlic and whole spices. It was first made by the royal Marwari cooks for the royal hunting party.

Kairi ki Sabzi: A delicious dish that will give you both salty and tangy flavours, Kairi ki Sabzi is a speciality of Rajasthani cuisine and the name itself will make your mouth water. This tangy side dish recipe is prepared using raw mangoes, which are known as Kairi in Hindi and are found in abundance in the summer season. An array of flavours are added in this curry with local spices, Kairi ki Sabzi is loved by people on a large scale. The jaggery added in the dish elevates the taste of the dish to another level and gives us a tangy, spicy and sweet experience in each bite. This dish tastes best when paired with hot, fresh rotis and also with boiled rice.

Haldi ki Sabzi: is a traditional Rajasthani recipe served on special occasions along with other traditional vegetables. This authentic side dish recipe is prepared by following simple steps and does not require much effort from your side. It can taste scrumptious when coupled with cooked rice, hot chapatis or even parathas. This dish is made by using simple ingredients like grated turmeric and yoghurt which makes this recipe simply hard to resist. It is apt to serve on the occasions like kitty party, potluck, buffet or on a family get-together.

Wholewheat Malpua: is a traditional Rajasthani recipe which is prepared with wholemeal flour, fennel seeds, sugar, ghee and peppercorns. This delectable dessert recipe is apt to serve on special occasions and festivals. Your kids would love to have this dessert after a hearty dinner or lunch. This dish has an unforgettable taste and is generally prepared in winters in Rajasthani households.

Makki Paneer Pakoda: is an easy-to-make pakoda recipe, which owes it's origin to Rajasthan. This delicious pakora is made using corns, gram flour (besan), paneer, garlic paste, ginger paste, green chili paste and a perfect combination of spices. This lip-smacking pakoda recipe is a twist to your usual paneer pakoda, which is now blended with the delectable flavors of corns. This snack recipe can compliment your tea and coffee really well. Serve hot with ketchup or chutney of your choice.

CHAPTER FOUR

Kashmiri Food Festival

Kashmir is famous all around the world for it's mouth-watering, flavorsome and royal Kashmiri Cuisines cuisine popularly known as 'Wazwan'. Wazwan is a multi-course meal with different varieties of vegetarian and non-vegetarian dishes. (predominantly mutton-based dishes). Wazwan is usually savored in Kashmiri weddings, gatherings, reunions, and food festivals and can include up to thirty-six delectable dishes. The word Wazwan is taken from two Kashmiri words 'Waz' meaning Cook or Chef and 'Wan' meaning shop. The Wazwan came to India in the 14th century when Timur a Mongol invader invaded India. At that time, India was ruled by Mughal Emperor, Nasiruddin Muhammad of Tughlaq dynasty. During this period lot of trained weavers, artisans, architects, woodcarvers, and cooks migrated to Kashmir from Samarkand, and the descendants of these cooks came to be known as Wazas, who are the traditional master chefs of Wazwan Cuisine. The infusion of tradition and culture lead to a beautiful amalgamation which we can see in the Wazwan dishes. The method of cooking for Wazwan includes Iranian, Afghan and Central Asian methods.

How is Wazwan Served?

Wazwan is served in copper plate/thali called Trammi or Traem. Usually, 4 people share this one Traem. Wazwan food is cooked in a very special way. Preparation of Wazwan is an art. The Wazwan is prepared by the chef known as 'Waza'. nowadays it is actually the availability of the Waza that determines the marriage schedule of Kashmiri wedding. The Wazwan is cooked in copper vessels which are plated with nickel. The food in these vessels is cooked over firewoods. Among thirty-six meals, fifteen preparations of meat are cooked overnight under the guidance of a head chef called Vast Waza. The Wazwan food contains a lot of dry fruits and it uses spices which are freshly homemade rather than the ones available in markets. Most of the Kashmiri cuisine is red in color which is usually derived from either the Kashmiri chilies or Cockscomb flower called Mawal. Before serving the food the washing of hands takes place in a special way. People wash their hands in Trash Naer which is brought by Waza or the close relatives join him in serving. Trash near is a copper vessel with a copper jug with the help of which guests wash their hands. A typical Wazwan Traem consists of rice and multi-course dishes. As it may be served pre-plated, the meal is consumed in a specific order. Starting from the Tabak Maaz, Methi Maaz, and the Seekh kebab and follow it up with the Rista, furthermore some more meat items, such as Rogan josh.

The culture of Kashmir is a blend of multiple customs and came from Northern India, Northern Pakistan and the Chinese territory of Aksai Chin. The state enjoys the presence of mix religions and that's why Kashmir is famous for its cultural heritage. It amalgamates Hindu, Sikh, Muslim and Buddhist people who make Kashmir more beautiful by adopting their own culture that has brought many changes in their living style.

Wazwan and their culture is highly influenced by Central Asian and Persian culture. Their dance, music, cuisine, carpet weaving and Koshur Sufiana forms a significant part of Kashmiri identity. Kashmiri culture is mainly followed by people living in Kashmir valley and Dodab of the Chenab region. The valley is known for the fine arts including traditional boats and houseboats, handicrafts and poetry.

The costume of Kashmiri people is very colorful and attractive. The majority of people wear traditional costume and women attire themselves with gorgeous jewelry like nose ring, bangles, earrings, necklaces and lose salwar kamiz which make them comfortable during the hot season. Whereas, men dress themselves in kurta pajama, shalwars, gurabi and skullcaps. Pheran is kind of overcoat wore by Kashmiri people during winter which is decorated with colorful patches and embroidery work. Most of the costumes of Kashmiri people are loose gown and it just varies in quality of fabric according to the weather. Most of the men wear headgear and women wear a skullcap. Most of the women cover their head and shoulders from strangers and elders as a matter of respect. The Kashmiri costume truly indicates their culture and lifestyle. It also shows that India is still following their cultural values.

Kashmir is a popular place for their beautiful and unique Handicraft. The Pashmina Shawl is famous worldwide for its quality and fabric. Almost every woman love and desire Pashmina Shawl as it symbolizes royalty. The design and embroidery work on the shawl is breathtaking also, the warmth and softness that it offers is completely matchless. Kashmir is also famous for their hand-knotted carpets and woolen rugs having floral design. On the other hand, basketry, paper mache, wooden carving furniture made of walnut wood and silverware are one of the best handicrafts offered by Kashmiri people.

Labbi Kabab: It is a meat dish which is flattened and given diamond shaped. It is also cooked in spices and yogurt. Succulent skewered lamb kebabs that go perfectly with some green chutney and onion ringlets. A delicious recipe to cook on festivals such as Eid or as a starter dish at a get-together with friends and family.

Rista: These are meatballs served in red gravy typically red in color. A Traem consists of 4 Ristas one for each person. To add color to Rista "Moval" a dried flower present only in Kashmir is used or we can also use saffron. The Rista or Meatballs are made by boneless meat which is smoothened on a wooden mallet. The Ristas often have meat fat which is added while the meat is smoothened. It requires the extraordinary skill that is reasons why it is made by the Wazas.

Rogan Josh: This is also Meat dish in which lamb is cooked in oil and Kashmiri spices. The color of the dish comes from Kashmiri Red Chillies added to it. To prepare Rogan josh the lamb or mutton meat needs to be marinated at least 2 hours before and then it is cooked in oil with other species.

Methi Korma: It is a sort of stew usually made with lamb stomach and flavored with methi or fenugreek leaves. This fenugreek (methi) flavored gravy is very famous amongst Kashmiris and part of the extensive meat cuisine of the region. The fenugreek leaves add a lovely flavor and the medium chopped meat goes yummy with either chapattis or rice. Serve methi Maaz to your family. They will love this delicious and unique dish

Palak Korma: This is a mutton dish cooked in a lot of Palak (Spinach). The aroma in the korma is because of the species infused with Palak and has silky consistency is because of it.

Tabak- Maaz: Tabakh Maaz is a glossy meat made of lamb ribs that are cooked twice and then simmered in yogurt with spices till tender. It's then fried thoroughly and served in dry form. The richness of the dish is apparent with the ingredient list, it tastes absolutely fabulous and the aroma pulls you towards another bite.

Yakhni: This dish can be prepared with lamb or lotus stem. It is a yogurt based dish cooked in yogurt and spices without chilies. Bay leaves, cloves, cardamoms are the prime flavors to the dish. In yakhni mutton is cut in the form of chunks of about.5-6 cm which is then pre-cooked in boiling water for 20 mins then the gravy of yogurt is added.

Ghustaba: It is the finishing dish. It is a dish of minced mutton balls which are made in yogurt and spices. It is similar to Rista but less spicy than that and aroma resembles with yakhni. Gustaba is like Rista made from pounded meat emulsion. The only difference lies in the way they are cooked.

Aab Gosh: This a mild dish, this is basically a dish in sheep ribs are cooked in milk, saffron, and cardamoms without spices. Basically in aab gosh, a sacral area of the vertebral column of lamb or mutton is cooked in milk.

Waza Chamman: This is a cheese dish. Cheese is called Chamman in Kashmiri. It this dish, cheese is cooked in tomato sauce along with spices.

Along with these dishes curd, pickle and chutney are served in small pots. The chutney can be of walnut, onion, pumpkin, radish etc. The Wazwan food ends with Phirni. It is a dessert made of sooji and milk served when cool and is garnished with lots of dry fruits and is very creamy and delicious.

Modur Pulav: It is the name given to sweetened Kashmiri rice prepared using cinnamon, a little guchhi, saffron, milk, ghee,sugar, cashew nuts, almonds, green cardamom among several other ingredients. This dish is sweet, flavoured and healthy with saffron as the main spice which gives it beautiful colour and taste.

Muji Gaad It is a dish made up of fish prepared generally with radish or nadur. This dish is an amalgamation of vegetarian and non-vegetarian items as the taste of fish and lotus stem blend together to give it a unique taste while hot spices and herbs add to it‘s unique yet amazing flavour and aroma.

Nadur Churma is one such delicacy involving the lotus stem. These fried lotus stems give the classic French fries a run for their money. Being rich in protein these are the most favorite past time snacks of the Kashmiri.

Paba It is made using peas and wheat. The dough is made using roasted flours of wheat, barley, buckwheat, peas and Ladakhi black beans, which makes it edible.

Paneer Chaman Cottage cheese or paneer cooked in milk until soft and tender

Pao Gogji Waters of turnips cooked in dry spices.

Phirni It is made of rice, milk, saffron, cardamom etc. Dry fruits and rose essence are also added to give it special flavor. The dessert gets its real flavor or taste with the delicacy with which the rice is ground. They are served in traditional earthen bowls called _shikoras'

Quabargah Ribs of young lamb or goat is cooked in a special blend of milk and spices, and then fried in ghee

Rajmaa Gogji Rajmash cooked with turnip

Rista Hand-pounded lamb in a red, red chilli-saffronfennel spice gravy coloured with ratanjoth, popular amongst Kashmiris

Roth It is type of roti that is sweet and made of flour ghee and sugar. The Kashmiri make it during auspicious days. The Kashmiri pundits make it during auspicious days as a ritual.

Sarvari Rice with black gram, chick peas or peas.

Sheer Chai Sheer Chai also known as Noon Chai or Pink Tea, is a traditional tea beverage of Kashmir. It is made of special tea leaves and a pinch of baking soda to give it a more pronounced pink color. It is slightly salty in taste.

Shufta Shufta is Kashmiri dessert that is made up of a lot of dry fruits and sugar

Kiyur It is made of loosely kneaded leavened wheat flour (only maida). It is spread over the Tawa so that it assumes a jelly like form of bread. It is taken with sugar and yoghurt.

Kulcha Kind of a bread prepared with Maida and wheatflour, the Kashmiri have it with morning tea. Dogris take this in all meals,

Lavash It is cream colored unleavened Armenian bread. It is mostly topped with sesame seeds or poppy seeds. This bread has a very unique taste as it is baked in a tandoor.

Khambir It is a pan-shaped local bread with a thick crust made from local whole wheat and it is served with butter tea which is prepared by adding salt and butter to tea.

Khamira, Pathoru and Thothru Wheat flour is kneaded and leavened with yeast (khamir) and then baked on tawa. Khamira is taken with ghee or butter. Pathorus have poopy seeds, coriander seeds and peeled almonds. Thothrus are globular in shape and smaller in size, preparation is same.

Khatta Meat Mutton cooked in tangy flavor achieved either by adding anardana (pomegranate seeds) or amchur (dry mango) powder.

Khurbani ka metha Dried apricots are soaked in water and simmered in sugar syrup and mildly flavored with saffron.

Ambal Pumpkin cooked in tangy sweet and sour taste by using tamarind or mango powder ot pomegranate seed along with jaggary.

Auria It is prepared by grinding sarson (mustard) seeds or rai into a fine powder and mixed with yoghurt and turmeric. It is then churned for some time and kept aside for fermentation. The slices of boiled and peeled potatoes or pumpkin are added to it. It is a pungent and digestive dish taken mostly with cooked rice.

Baqer Khani This dish is a kind of Kashmiri puff pastry. It is a type of soft naan sprinkled with sesame seeds.

Kahva is a herbal green tea brewed with saffron spices, almonds, and walnut. Whenever there is a feast or festival, Kahva is served. You will find 20 different variations of Kahvah since it is made in every household. Some people also prefer to put milk in it.

Shab Deg is a meat delicacy cooked overnight with patience and richness of ingredients. Shab means night and Deg is a large cooking vessel. A rooster is cooked with turnips and spices overnight to bring out the right flavors in the dish and the vessel is sealed with dough. It is a special dish made for large families or when you are having people over.

Lyader Tschaman is a Kashmiri cottage cheese cooked in rich creamy gravy. The cottage cheese in Kashmir is yellow in color and so is the gravy. You will find this dish in almost every household. A traditional delicacy even non-vegetarians won't be able to stop themselves from relishing. Undoubtedly, it is the most sought-after vegetarian Kashmiri food.

Kashmiri dahi baingan is one of the tasty and unique lip smacking dish made in spices which you simply can't resist. The eggplant is diced and cooked in a yoghurt gravy which make you want more of the dish. It is a perfect Kashmir food fusion served as a side dish. This vegetarian dish which can be cooked in several ways is equally loved by the people of Kashmir.

Thukpa is an extremely scrumptious dish that originated from the Eastern part of Tibet. Made with thick noodles submerged in a delectable vegetable soup, Thukpa is every local's favorite in Kashmir. Offering a great amalgamation of noodles and soup, this dish can either be served vegetarian or non-vegetarian and appeals to every foodie's soul out there.

Khambir is a must-try dish for those travelers who are seeking to try something unique. Eaten during breakfast, Khambir is a bread that is brown in color and has a thick crust. It is made from local whole wheat and makes the diners crave for more and more.

Nadir Monji is a flavorsome Kashmir Food that is perfect for all those who love fried and spicy dishes. Made from Lotus stem, Nadir Monji is one of the favorite snacks of all the locals in Kashmir. To prepare this dish, Lotus stem is covered with a paste of gram flour and spices and then deep-fried. Served with mint dip, Nadir Monji will surely kill your hunger pangs while you are exploring the Dal Lake.

Bazbatta Kashmiri vegetable pulao

Butter Tea It is prepared by adding butter and salt to tea, sometimes pieces of yak meat are also added to it.

Dum Aloo Kashmir food style: The baby potatoes are cooked in yogurt, ginger paste, fennel, and hot spices. Just the aroma of this simple dish is appetizing. Have it with roti or naan bread.

Modur Pulao is not the regular Pulao dish that your mother gives you in the tiffin. It is prepared in the goodness of milk, saffron, ghee, and cinnamon. That's not it! The rice is then garnished with a whole lot of dry fruits like almonds, cashews, and raisins.

Chaang Tibetan alcoholic beverage made either by barley, rice or millet.

CHAPTER FIVE

Hawaiian Seafood Festival

Hawaiian theme have one element in common — the colorful theme. Here's how to create your own tropical paradise with some fun decorations.

Giant Pineapple Paper Lanterns : Wow your guests with giant paper lanterns that suit your Hawaiian theme party. Look for fun, tropical motifs like pineapples, coconuts, palm trees, and hibiscus flowers. If your party is indoors, hang your paper lanterns from the ceiling — they look especially festive over a table display or at the entrance to your party venue.

Tropical Flower Garlands: It wouldn't be a Hawaiian theme party without the appearance of some gorgeous tropical flowers. Flower garlands are a simple way to add pops of color to your Hawaiian theme as they're easy to source or make.

Tiki Torches: Light the way for your guests to your island paradise with some tiki torches. These tall, rustic torches really amp up the atmosphere of your tropical party. Tiki torches create a lovely, warm glow and are perfect for outdoor luaus. (Just make sure you keep the area around the torches clear of potential hazards.)

Inflatable Palm Trees with beach layout: Inflatable palm trees surrounded beach to add a touch of fun to your Hawaiian theme.

Attire and Music: If everyone in Aloha attire is a feast for the eyes, then Hawaiian music will be a feast for the ears. An easy way to create a festive tropical vibe is to play Hawaiian or island party music over a decent boom box, computer or MP3 player speakers or a component sound system. Traditional Hawaiian music will create a more enchanting ambiance while contemporary music will create more of a festive ambiance.

Tropical Drinks – Tasty tropical drinks are the lifeblood of your party. All you need is a little mai tai mix from your nearby supermarket, ice, rum and a blender. Add some colorful flare with some punch syrup and add a drink umbrella and some sliced pineapple. And if you don't really feel like trying, just go old school with some coconut rum and Coke. It's better than nothing.

Poi – Perhaps the food most associated with Hawaii is poi. Some people like it. Some people don't. If you are afraid that poi will gross for your friends to handle, then substitute it with sweet potatoes or rice. Both are commonly served at luaus in Hawaii.

Mahi Mahi or other Fish – Fish is another common luau staple. The easy thing to do is get some frozen mahi mahi fillets from your local supermarket then bake them in the oven and serve it with tartar sauce. Costco has usually has an assortment of frozen fish fillets to choose from.

Lomi Lomi Salmon – This dish consists of salted salmon, diced raw tomatoes, onions and green onions all mixed together. Many people put lomi lomi salmon recipe in their poi to give it more flavor. This dish also adds some vibrant color to your spread.

Lau lau – This is another popular dish but it is also really hard to make. It is made of Mutton, pork or fish and taro wrapped in ti leaves and banana leaves then steamed for hours until the ti leaves because super soft. If you are hardcore, make this. If you aren't hardcore, buy it. If it's not available to buy, skip it.

Haupia – This is a yummy coconut putting made of coconut milk, sugar and starch. If that sounds like rocket science to you, then we suggest you just order powdered haupia mix over the Internet. Just add water. It's easier than making brownies.

Poke (poh-keh) - Poke is raw fish seasoned with salt, seaweed, onions and some other oils and spices. Think of it as sashimi cubes mixed with a bunch of stuff. If your friends don't like sashimi and sushi, they probably won't like poke.

CHAPTER SIX

Sri Lankan Food Festival

Sri Lanka's religious heritage has been largely influenced by the tradition of Buddhism, as well as a smaller population of Hindus, while its mingled history of colonialism has created a unique culture of music, dance and arts, not to mention sports. As most would know, cricket is a wildly popular sport in Sri Lanka, with the national cricket team held in high revere and the sport playing an important role in everyday life. The sport arrived not long after the British, with the first game thought to have been played as far back as 1800. As for wellbeing, Sri Lanka is renowned for having one of the highest qualities of life in the developing world. A large part of their medical tradition stems from the South Asian Ayurvedic practices. The tradition of Ayurveda, which links illness with imbalance in the body, includes practices like aromatherapy, herbal medicine, acupuncture, yoga, massage, meditation and balancing of energies.

Sri Lankans have three official languages: Sinhala, Tamil and English. Sinhala, the language of the majority, and Tamil, spoken by ethnic Tamils as well as Muslims, are the primary languages of the island, with English introduced during the British occupation. The nation's three major ethnic groups are represented in the block colours on the flag, while the symbol of the elephant marks national heritage and prosperity.

Sri Lankan cuisine is an ode to spices and age-old techniques: Home to time-honored traditional cuisine, Sri Lanka is a marvelous country for those wanting to dig uninfluenced ancient flavors. The mouth-melting food of the island seizes your imagination with its spices, curries, and techniques. Spot on! Besides being flavourful, the rich cuisine of Sri Lanka is also a recollection of the multicultural values it shares with India. Tamil flavors continue to conquer taste buds; coconut is a staple and plays a crucial part in almost every dish; Sinhalese cuisine will never fail to surprise you with its sundry oddments. Sri Lanka still maintains the culinary intricacies of its food fortes by using principal spices and time-worn techniques from the time of the Vellalas. Centuries later, in attendance, the locals still focus on cooking with fresh ingredients, establishing culinary dominance with a precise blend of herbs, vegetables, rice, seafood and fruits. But if you want to taste authentic Ceylon cuisine in its original form, you need to visit some of the local restaurants tucked away on quiet streets. It is hard to steer clear of these age-old recipes when Sri Lanka presents them to you the way it does. Here are a few authentic dishes from Sri Lanka to tickle your taste buds.

Gotu Kola Mallum Sambola – Shredded Greens With Coconut: This Sri Lankan cuisine is like a healthy green salad prepared by mixing shredded green vegetables, basic spices available, coconut, chilli, onion, and Umbalakada fish. Enjoy this green leafy and spicey vegetable dish with some steaming hot white rice in an afternoon meal.

Ingredients used: green vegetables, green chilli, onion, coconut, and Umbalakada fish

Eaten with: rice & curry dishes

Polos – A Spicy Dish Of Jackfruit: Spices are dry roasted, small pieces of jackfruit are mixed with the roasted spices. Mustard seed oil is heated in a pan, and garlic, onion, curry leaves, lemongrass and cinnamon are added. Then jackfruit pieces are mixed with the gravy and coconut mix is poured. Its then cooked for an hour.

Ingredients used: Jackfruit, cinnamon, curry leaves, spices, garlic, lemongrass, onion, mustard seeds, and coconut milk.

Eaten with: Rice and Parippu

Parippu – Spicy Lentil: Are you ready for a flavorsome **Sri Lankan curry**- This delicious Sri Lankan cuisine is prepared using boiled red lentils. Curry leaves, onion, spices, and garlic are added to hot oil, and the curry is cooked until it turns yellow. This flavorsome and creamy daal or parippu curry will make your simple steamed rice taste heavenly.

Ingredients used: red and yellow lentils, spices, onion, curry leaves, coconut milk, and garlic.

Eaten with: rice and wambatu moju

Wambatu Moju – An Eggplant Pickle: Sri lankan cuisine is a highly flavoured side dish prepared by cutting eggplant in wedges and deep-frying them to give crispy texture. Then its caramelized with sugar, vinegar, green chillies, red onions, and mustard seeds.

Ingredients used: eggplant, spices, oil, vinegar, onion, green chillies, and sugar.
Eaten with: plain rice and roasted paan

Fish Ambul Thiyal – A Saporous Fish Dish: This is one of the easiest **Sri Lankan cuisine recipes** when it comes to preparation. Fishes are cut into cubes and then sauteed in an aromatic blend of spices. It is then cooked until the little water is reduced. Savor this tasty Fish Thiyal for a burst of flavours inside your mouth.

Ingredients used: pandan leaves, curry leaves, oil, spices, a large & firm fish, and dried goraka.
Eaten with: roasted paan or theti paan

Kottu – Sri Lankas Hamburger: A popular Sri Lankan cuisine, Kottu is prepared using a flat crispy bread called godamba roti. The roti is deep fried and chopped, and then vegetables and spices are added to the mix. The preparation is served with spicy curry sauce. Does this remind of pasta- Make sure you taste it to know whether it also tastes like pasta.

Ingredients used: godamba roti, spices, and vegetables.
Eaten with: spicy curry sauce

Kukul Mas Curry – A Flavorsome Curry: Spices are fried in oil, coconut milk and tomato puree are added. Chicken pieces are then added to the thick gravy and stewed for a while. It tastes best with rice and bread. This is a popular Sri Lankan cuisine in Colombo. Enjoy this yummy chicken curry with plain rice for the best taste.

Ingredients used: spices, curry leaves, lemongrass, pandan leaves, oil, coconut milk, and chicken.
Eaten with: plain rice or theti paan

Lamprais – Meat Marinated In Sambal Chili Sauce: This Sri Lankan cuisine is a flavourful dish eaten with rice. Meat, rice, and sambal chili sauce are wrapped in a banana leaf packet to steam. This process adds a special flavor of the banana leaf to it which increases the taste of the dish. The rice is cooked with meat stock and then served with the meat curry on a banana leaf.

Ingredients used: Oil, spices, meat, beef/pork/lamb stock, and rice.
Eaten with: Rice

Sri Lankan Egg Hoppers – Pancakes For Breakfast: A fermented concoction of rice flour, coconut milk, and a hint of sugar is used to make the batter. The batter is cooked in a small wok and swirled around to even it out. An egg is cracked into the bowl-shaped pancake and garnished with chilies, lunu miris, onions, lemon juice, and salt.

Ingredients used: egg, chillies, lemon juice, lunumiris, oil, flour and coconut milk for batter.

Eaten with: spicy chile sauce, dhaal curry, and chutney

Kiribath – Tasty Combo Of Rice And Coconut Milk: Kiribath is a dish which is prepared during the special occasions in Sri Lanka. The dish is prepared by boiling the rice and cooking it with coconut milk and a pinch of salt. Once the consistency of the mix becomes sticky, it is left to set. Then the mixture is cut into slices. Kiribath is popularly garnished with lunu miris, a kind of traditional chili sauce.

Ingredients used: Rice, Coconut milk, salt

Eaten with: lunu miris

Idiyappam (String Hoppers): The batter is poured into a specialized utensil and squeezed into noodle-like strings, which are then steamed. String hoppers require plenty of practice and patience to achieve the ideal consistency. String hoppers pair wonderfully well with beef curry, chicken curry, dhal, sambol, and many other dishes. Often, when eating them with curries and sambol

Pol Sambol (Spicy Coconut Relish): One of Sri Lanka's simplest dishes to prepare, pol sambol is a Sri Lankan-style relish, made from shredded coconut, chili powder, sliced onions, and lime juice. pol sambol is commonly eaten with fresh bread, hoppers, or a side of rice. Some Sri Lankans also enjoy it with Maldive fish, a cured tuna fish.

Lunu Miris (Onion Chili Mix): Lunu miris is another quick, go-to dish in Sri Lanka. It only requires a few minutes to prepare, and it is made from a handful of simple ingredients: salt, chili, and onion. Sometimes, lunu miris is served with Maldive fish, to add freshness and saltiness to the dish. Served together, this Sri Lankan favorite pairs wonderfully with both appas and hot peppers.

Kalu Pol Wattakka (Pumpkin Curry): Kalu pol wattakka is a diverse pumpkin-based curry, with a wide range of variations. The creamy pumpkin curry, however, is one of the country's most beloved versions. While not a popular ingredient in Sri Lankan cooking, pumpkin is very much the star of this unique dish. The pumpkin is cooked in a creamy curry sauce, with a gravy-like consistency, which is made by first roasting shredded coconut and rice, and then adding them into a curry-base with coconut milk. Kalu pol wattakka, in particular, has a truly sweet and alluring aroma.

Wambatu Moju (Eggplant Curry): A curry with plenty of richness and acidity, wambatu moju is a Sri Lankan dish that brings a range of textures and flavors to the plate. It is made by deep-frying sliced eggplant in plenty of oil, then stir-frying the eggplant with green chili, onion, and a range of spices. Before serving, the mixture is left to rest in a bowl of sugar and vinegar to truly let the flavors meld and mature. Although classed as a curry, wambatu moju is far closer to pickle in its preparation and taste. Each mouthful explodes with sweet, spicy, and sour notes, making it one of the most unique foods to try in Sri Lanka.

Annasi Curry (Pineapple Curry): A curry of pineapple and various spices, the balance of sweet and savory in this striking and flavorsome dish is perfect for those who prefer milder, sweeter curries. Served with rice, or eaten on its own, annasi curry is one of the hidden gems of Sri Lankan cuisine. It may raise some eyebrows, but it is packed with flavor.

Malu Ambul Thiyal (Sour Fish Curry): Sour fish curry is Sri Lankan specialty, and one of the country's must-try dishes. Many Sri Lankans go crazy for this curry, and after a single mouthful, you'll no doubt understand why. The fish is cooked in a customized spice mix of black pepper and goraka (garcinia cambogia), which not only helps preserve the mixture for up to a week but also contributes to the depth and unique flavor of this seafood dish. Malu ambul thiyal is a dish that has been passed down through generations of Sri Lankans, and it is widely believed the recipe has not changed from its humble origins.

Wattalapan (Famous Pudding): wattalapan is the next best thing that unites Sri Lankans. It is a food integral to Sri Lankan culture and one of the most popular dishes enjoyed during Eid festival, which marks the end of the fasting throughout Ramadan. Undoubtedly the country's most popular dessert, wattalapan is renowned for its silky texture and fragrant aroma. A pudding with the melt-in-mouth consistency of marshmallows, it is made from a combination of sugar, coconut milk, ground nutmeg, vanilla extract, ground cinnamon, ground cardamom, eggs, and cashews. Truly indulgent, with both sweet and spiced notes in every bite, the soft texture of this wonderous dessert alone will have you coming back for more, let alone the taste.

Lavariya: A traditional dessert and a great source of pride for Sri Lankans, lavariya is the perfect sweet snack for breakfast, with tea, or following a hearty main. Delicious when gobbled down fresh from a hot pan, lavariya is a wholesome dessert made from rice flour, shredded coconut, jaggery, cardamom, water, and oil. Making lavariya is something of an art form, and many home chefs perfect this dish over weeks and months, crafting it with passion to create a dish of such elegance and beauty.

KOTHU ROTI: Sri Lanka's most popular street food choice – Soft, flaky paratha flat bread chopped into strips and stir-fried together with crispy mixed veg, fried egg and a fiery mix of authentic spices

CHAPTER SEVEN

Punjabi Food Festival

Tandoori Chicken: Tandoori chicken is a Punjabi cuisine which is also known as tandoori murgh. The chicken meat is mixed in yogurt seasoned with tandoori masala, nutmeg, and cumin seeds before being skewered. Traditionally, this Punjabi food is cooked at high temperatures in tandoors to give a smoky flavor.

Butter Chicken: Butter chicken in India is a favorite Indian meal that combines chicken, spices, tomatoes, and cream. Classic butter chicken has delicious creamy gravy. The juicy chicken is served with basmati rice or naan bread.

Sarson Ka Saag – One Of The Most Famous Punjabi Foods: Sarson ka saag (a vegetarian Punjabi specialty) is one of the most traditional and popular vegetarian dishes of Punjab. Punjabis prepare it in desi ghee which is later served with makki ki roti (makki di roti.)

Paneer Tikka – The Famous Dish: The paneer tikka, sometimes known as "vegetarian chicken," holds a unique position in Punjabi cuisine. When it comes to vegetarian appetizers, this soft cottage cheese delicacy, chargrilled, is the first that comes to mind. Generally speaking, Punjabi food fits quite well into the vegetarian diet.

Rajma Chawal: Rajma Chawal is a must-have in every north Indian household and a source of nostalgia for many. Even though it originates in Kashmir, it is a favorite in Indian Punjabis. This meal is usually served with a side of pickled onions.

Amritsari Fish: All fish lovers will enjoy this. Beautiful pieces of fish, deep-fried to golden perfection and coated in a spiced batter. The Fish is then garnished with lemon juice and a coating of garam masala for additional zing.

Dal Makhani -Traditional Punjabi Foods: This rich mixture of black lentils and red kidney beans is a delightful buttery Punjabi lentil meal. It is served in a thick gravy with platefuls of cream to make it richer. It is a buttery food dish fit for a royal court.

Chana Masala: This traditional North Indian style curry is also known as Chole Masala. It is cooked with white chickpeas, freshly powdered spices, onions, tomatoes, and herbs. To enhance the taste of this Punjabi chickpea curry, it is prepared in desi ghee using a different ghee recipe. Thus, this spicy chickpea curry could be a favorite dish of traditional Punjabi food lovers at an unexpected dinner party.

Chicken Tikka – One Of The Most Delicious Punjabi Foods: Chicken Tikka is a flavourful and colorful Indian chicken dish that is traditional and popular. Chicken is marinated with the paste of garlic cloves and some spices. After that, the ground meat is grilled hot and served to eat. Chicken tikka has become so famous you can go to any European city and find a restaurant that serves this dish.

Punjabi Kadhi Pakoda: The Punjabi Kadhi confirms the awesomeness of Punjab's everyday food. Besan pakoras are deep-fried in ghee before being added into kadhi. Gram flour (besan) and onions make Pakora for Kadhi.

Chicken Curry – Punjabi Dhaba Style : Chicken curry cooked in different spices is the perfect Punjabi recipe for meat lovers. Boneless chicken pieces mixed with ginger garlic paste, green chilies, and tomatoes make for the best dish.

People often add red chili powder to the juicy chicken pieces to make the food spicy. It is served with Tandoori roti. In Punjabi households' tandoori roti is the preferable side dish.

Punjabi Bharwa Karele (Bitter gourd) - This stay good for long time without refrigeration. So my grandma used to cook this with chapattis for travelling.

Chole Bhature: Chole Bhature, also called Chana Bhatura, is one of the most popular Punjabi dishes enjoyed almost across the entire nation. While Chole refers to a spicy and tangy chickpea curry, Bhatura stands for soft and fluffy fried leavened bread. Chole Bhature is thus a spicy, tasty and fulfilling dish. Each restaurant or dhaba has its own flavor and taste in chickpea curry. While the curry is very spicy at some places, at others it may have a tangy taste. Moreover, even the curry's consistency varies from slightly thick to semi-dry and dry. Talking about the bhatura, its size and flavor also vary from one restaurant to another. Preferably, a bhatura should not be too oily and puff fully. A piece of advice, eat them hot and fresh, as they turn limp and dense if taken in a parcel.

Amritsari Kulcha: Amritsari Kulcha is a typical Punjabi flatbread prepared with all-purpose flour or maida with potato stuffing. Amritsari naan or kulcha is typically prepared in an Indian tandoor oven but can also be cooked over a tawa on the stovetop. It is generally consumed with chole masala or chana masala but can also be enjoyed without a complimentary dish because of its stuffing.

Mango Lassi: Mango lassi is a delicious Indian drink made with mangoes, curd, milk, and sugar. When Indian mangoes are in season, mango lassi is popular. Punjabi mango lassi keeps the body cool throughout the hot summer months. A lot of people like to add a form of alcohol to drink at night time with their meal.

Spicy Chickpea Wraps: Spicy chickpea wraps with avocado and spinach are tasty and quick to prepare. Boiled chickpeas wrapped in Indian flatbread tastes amazing. Whole wheat flour roti can also make a chickpea wrapper.

Panjiri : Panjiri is the most traditional Punjabi sweet dish among all Punjabi sweet dishes. It is prepared with butter, sugar, cardamom, and almonds roasted in flour.

Chitt : This gravy made up of ginger-garlic was a common dish that was cooked in many Punjabi households. Known for its immunity-boosting benefits, this dish was also considered a perfect remedy for sore throat. This dish has milk or curd which gives it a creamier texture.

Shikar Da Aachar : India has a special love for pickles. This non-vegetarian pickle is made up of quail meat, vinegar, mustard oil, and so many other spices. This pickle has lost its significance these days but needs to be revived. Using vinegar is quite essential in this pickle as it helps in increasing the pickle's shelf life.

Ganne Wale Chawal : Also known as raawh wale chaawal in Punjab and rasawal in old Lucknow, this is actually a slow-cooked dish in which rice is cooked on low flame with sugarcane juice and later garnished with nuts. Earlier it was cooked in Lohri celebrations but now has lost its significance.

Phulkari Pulao : This rich dish is connected to the regime of Maharaja Ranjit Singh in Patiala. Made with curd and khoya, this dish has beautiful spots and thus, resembles Phulkari. When garnished with dry fruits and pomegranate seeds, this dish can show you a really good time.

Mutton Taka Tak : There are so many mutton dishes from Punjab that we absolutely love. This is one such mutton delicacy that is absolutely delicious and thus needs the limelight. These crispy mutton cutlets with sprinkled garam masala and whole coriander were commonly sold as street food in Punjab but now have got lost.

Chaat Wala Garam Masala: Made with a higher quantity of jeera that overpowers the dhania, saunf and elaichi ingredients, this version is used for dahi bhallas, chaats and tikkis on average Punjabi homes. The jaiphal and javitri are also small quantities to up the spicy taste. This is used in minimal amounts as a spice mix for chaat-based anything.

Achari Style Garam Masala: Up the saunf in the garam masala mix, and you get an achari style masala mix. This is best used in bhindi, dry potato preparations, and saute-style veggies. Stuffed veggies such as eggplant and water gourd too work well with this variant of garam masala. But, primarily, any veggie preparation that is tossed and fried finds awesomeness with this final garnish of garam masala in an achari avatar.

Gravy Style Garam Masala: Garam masala for the gravies use more green cardamom and go low on the jaiphal and javitri. However, this masala is also used in teeny bits across all pulao doses across Punjabi homes. The USP of this version of the garam masala is that the mix does not hit the tongue directly as it hits the nose.

Kadhai Style Garam Masala: Suppose you are looking for a masala to use in non-vegetarian dishes or items that need an excellent roast mix before being served. In that case, this essential garam masala high on dhania proportion is a must-have at home. This garam masala is rich in taste and has a slightly coarse texture. Overuse can make the entire dish bitter, but this garam masala mix can work wonders when used cleverly.

Phulkari: Phulkari Pulao is an aromatic, sweet, flavorful preparation of rice that uses an assortment of rice and vegetables and the richness of ghee, poppy seeds and saffron.

Phulkari pulao is very different from a normal pulao we eat at home or restaurant. I have listed down a few unique features of the pulao.

- Four different varieties of aromatic rice in a fixed ratio
- Richness of saffron and mawa
- Lavishness of poppy seeds
- Hand-churned ghee
- Pot-based cooking

You will find fried rice or veg pulao in every Indian kitchen but here is something more delicious and nutritious. It's a pulao made with three to four types of rice in a fixed proportion. It's basically cooked with ghee, milk, mawa and exotic spices like poppy seeds, saffron and other healthy vegetables. This pulao indeed is very colorful.

Kulfa:- Kulfa refers to the rich, mouthwatering dessert from the city of Amritsar. A large-sized kulfi is cut and fresh Rabri of rich flavor is added to it and add a generous amount of almond and pistachio. To make it tastier, it is served on top with Lachha and Falooda, Rabri, Some Crusade Ice, Gun Katira. This is one of the best alternatives to eating ice creams in summer.

Gobhi-Gajar-Shalgam Pickle: Tangy and spicy pickles will tingle your palates. One of the pickles most loved by all is Gobhi, Gajar, and Shalgam pickles. The blend of spicy and sweet flavours will stay with you for a long time!

CHAPTER EIGHT

Sattvik Food Festival

Sattvic is derived from sattva (सत्त्व) which is a Sanskrit word. Sattva is a complex concept in Indian philosophy, used in many contexts, and it means one that is pure, essence, nature, vital, energy, clean, conscious, strong, courage, true, honest, wise, rudiment of life.

Sattva is one of three gunas (quality, peculiarity, tendency, attribute, property). The other two qualities are considered to be rajas (agitated, passionate, moving, emotional, trendy) and tamas (dark, destructive, spoiled, ignorant, stale, inertia, unripe, unnatural, weak, unclean).

The three gunas

Ayurveda and Yoga are built on the philosophy of the three gunas: sattva, rajas and tamas. These concepts represent the qualities that are present in food, nature and actions, as well as our body and mind.

TAMAS: Tamas is inertia, darkness and dullness. When a seed is resting inert in the darkness of the earth, it is in a state of tamas. When we sleep, it is tamas. When tamas is dominant in our lives, there is heaviness, sleeping too much and eating leftovers, meat and deep-fried foods. It leads to lethargy, lack of purpose and depression.

RAJAS: Rajas is activity and movement. When a seedling cracks through the endosperm and pushes through the earth to reach the sun, it is in a state of rajas. When rajas is dominant in our lives, it looks like stimulation, stress and overexcitement. Too much rajas imbalances the body and mind, leading to anxiety, disturbed sleep and overindulgence.

SATTVA: Sattva is balance and harmony. When a seedling has turned into a beautiful flower, unfurling its petals to soak in the beauty of the sun, it is in a state of sattva. When sattva is present, it looks like lightness and grounding, peace and serenity in the body and mind. This is our ideal state, one that defines true health.

Sattvic foods

Sattvic foods are balancing and harmonious, and they are plentiful; this is only a partial list to have you think about the qualities and how they make you feel. Sattvic foods can be loosely categorized as most fresh fruits and vegetables, most whole grains, legumes and nuts. How they are eaten, for example cooked versus raw, can make a difference in whether they add sattva or rajas to the mind and body. A vegetable may have all of the possibility of sattva but if it is eaten raw then it may be rajas for the body and mind. Many fruits are also sattva for the body and mind when cooked lightly with ghee and spices. In all cases we are assuming food that is fresh, not genetically modified and without chemicals in the process of growing and delivery.

Fruits - apples, apricots, berries, dates (fresh), dragonfruit, feijjoa, figs, grapefruit, grapes with seeds, longons, lychee, kiwifruit, mangoes, melons, nectarine, oranges, peaches, pears, persimmon, pineapple, plums, pomegranates, prunes, starfruit, tangerines (sweet), raisins

Legumes - adzuki beans, anasazi beans, black beans, black eyed peas, broad beans, brown lentils, cannellini beans, edamame beans, fava beans, green lentils, lima beans, mung beans, fresh snap peas, split mung beans, split peas

Nuts - almonds, brazil nuts, cashew nuts cooked, chestnuts, coconut, filberts, gingko, hazelnuts, macadamia nuts, pine nuts, walnuts, pecans, pistachio, tahini, tiger nuts

Oils - almond oil, coconut oil, flaxseed oil, ghee, macadamia nut oil, mustard seed oil, sesame oil, olive oil

Other - honey, maple syrup, raw milk, raw sugar cane, watercress, fresh wasabi, ros

e petals, lavender flowers, fresh almond milk, fresh rice milk, fresh coconut water

Spices - anise, basil, black pepper, brown mustard seeds, cardamom, carob, cilantro, cinnamon, cumin, coriander, dill, fennel, ginger, mint, lemon grass, sesame seeds, sorrel, turmeric, vanilla bean

Vegetables - artichokes, asparagus, bamboo shoots, beets, bitter gourd, bok choy, broccoli, brussel sprouts, burdock, cabbage, carrots, cauliflower, celeriac, celery, corn, courgette (zucchini), cucumbers, daikon, fennel bulb, flowers (edible), green beans, dark leafy greens, jerusalem artichoke, kohlrabi, lotus root, okra, parsnips, snow peas, spinach, summer squash, sweet potatoes, turnips (sweet), yacon, yams

Whole grains - amaranth, barley, rice (high quality, basmati, jasmine...), buckwheat, cornmeal, farro, kamut, millet, oats, quinoa, rye, spelt, teff, wheat, wild rice, fresh pasta, fresh noodles.

Rajasic foods

Rajasic foods are stimulating and contribute to physical and mental stress. Small amounts of rajasic foods are not a problem in an otherwise balanced life, but a diet made up of too many rajasic foods overstimulates the body and mind and will lead to circulatory and nervous system disorders.

Fruits - dates (dried), bottled juices, guava, lime, lemon, passion fruit, papaya, soursop

Legumes - kidney beans, navy beans, pinto beans, red lentils

Nuts and seeds - hemp seeds, peanuts, sprouts, sunflower seeds

Oils - avocado oil, hemp oil, peanut oil, sunflower oil

Other - fresh cheeses, avocado, cottage cheese, egg, all fermented foods, ice cream, miso, molasses, sucanat, olives, salt, vinegar, yogurt, commercial almond, hemp or rice milk, all caffeine (including cacao, chocolate, coffee, caffeinated teas, decaf tea and coffee)

Spices - asafoetida/hing, cayenne, chili pepper, fenugreek, garlic, excess of any spice

Vegetables - eggplant, onions, capsicum (bell peppers), leeks, hot peppers (chilis), potatoes, radishes, sea vegetables, sprouts, tomatoes

Whole grains - Commercial rolled oats, parboiled grains

Tamasic foods

Tamasic foods are impure, rotten, or dead and create heaviness and lethargy physically, mentally, emotionally and spiritually. Eating tamasic food leads to dullness, lack of motivation and purpose and negativity.

Fruits - all over-ripe fruits, bananas

Grains - all exposed to light or more than one year old, extensively refined grains, dried and packaged pasta

Legumes - all canned, older than 2 years, garbanzo beans (chickpeas)

Nuts and Seeds - all old or exposed to light, chia seeds

Oils - all older than 1 year or rancid, canola oil, vegetable oil, rapeseed oil, safflower oil

Other - alcohol, all animal flesh (beef, chicken, fish, fowl, goat, lamb, pork, rabbit, shellfish, turkey, venison), artificial sweeteners, barbecued or blackened foods, food with preservatives or synthetic ingredients, deep fried foods, frozen foods, leftovers, margarine, condiments, all refined sugar, old tea bags, smoked food, microwaved food

Spices - all old or stored in the light

Vegetables - all mushrooms, pumpkin, winter squash.

FOODS TO BE AVOIDED

When on a sattvic diet do not eat - salty and sour foods, tea, coffee, alcohol, onions and garlic, frozen food, fast food, microwaved foods, processed foods, meat, fish, eggs and leftovers or previously prepared food.

Benefits of Sattvic Diet Yogic diet, or sattvic diet benefits the body, mind and soul in innumerable ways. Few of them are as follows .

• In the yogic diet, it is a rule to start the day with a glass of warm water with lemon juice in it. This cleanses the body and helps it to get rid of harmful toxins. By the process of regular detoxification, organs in the body can function well, as a result of which the body is devoid of ailments and diseases. • The satvik diet not only keeps one physically fit, but also mentally agile. It is a diet which balances the body, mind and soul, thereby resulting in longevity of life in an individual.

• The yoga diet believes in eating in moderation, therefore the yoga diet for weight loss is one of the best ways to lose fat, and it also strengthens your body's immunity power at the same time. Following the diet along with a few minutes of yoga, pranayama or some physical activity will keep you away from all types of lifestyle diseases like blood pressure, diabetes, etc.

• Sattvic diet includes green leafy vegetables, fruits and sprouts and is devoid of heat inducing foods like meat, fish, onion, garlic, etc. Therefore, it does not take much of hard work for the digestive system to digest the food; the end result of which is proper bowel movement, clear skin, etc.

• Sattvic foods include ghee, coconut oil, sprouted seeds, etc. These make the food tasty. Moreover, the good fats in the diet help in keeping your brain healthy and your memory sharp.

Homemade Yogurt: Yogurt is made by the bacterial fermentation of milk and is a popular dairy product. Yogurt cultures are fermented with natural sugars found in the milk. Fresh yogurt made at home has a high concentration of beneficial bacteria that helps with digestion and eliminates harmful viruses. Commercial yogurt available in the market is generally packed with sugar and other additives which are not good for the body.

Ghee (Clarified Butter): Ghee, also known as clarified butter, is made by heating unsalted butter until it clarifies and separates into lactose, fat, and milk protein. Heating on a low flame the sugar and protein separate and sink to the bottom. According to Ayurveda, Ghee reduces inflammation in the body, lubricates the connective tissues, promotes memory, intelligence, and enhances digestion, among other things. Also, its antioxidant properties boost the immune system. It also helps in digestion by allowing food to be broken down efficiently by stimulating the digestive enzymes.

Raw Honey: Honey is the longest-lasting of all sattvic foods. It is easy to digest and has great detoxification properties. But the most important point to note here is that the honey must be raw, organic, and free from preservatives. Ayurveda promotes the intake of honey with cold water. Honey should never be boiled or put in hot water. In fact, any process which involves the heating of honey is not favored by Ayurveda. Honey can be mixed with lemon juice and consumed empty stomach early morning. It regulates the secretion of internal glandular organs and helps with digestion. It is also used to treat a wide variety of problems such as constipation, insomnia, indigestion, anemia, and even used in the treatment of jaundice where it is mixed with Giloy (an immunity-boosting herb) and taken in orally.

Honey has a high antibacterial activity that helps in healing wounds, relieving sore throats, mouth ulcers, sore gums, and much more. Ayurveda also says that honey is useful in lowering cholesterol and weight loss. The assumption here is that it is taken in moderate quantities. Ayurveda recommends taking not more than 4 to 5 teaspoons of honey in a day. However, people suffering from high sugar conditions or diabetes should not consume honey. Honey should also not be mixed with hot milk. In case you have a medical condition, please consult an Ayurvedic doctor before consuming honey.

Whole Grains and Legumes: Grains are edible seeds of plants and are considered to be ‘whole grains’ when they contain all the three key parts of the seed: the bran, germ, and endosperm. Ayurveda recommends eating whole grains where all the parts of the seed are intact. All grains start as whole grains, but as they enter the markets, the key parts of the seed are stripped away in order to increase the shelf life of the product. This results in the loss of important nutrients from the grains.

Whole grains keep the heart healthy, control appetite, regulate blood pressure, and maintain healthy cholesterol levels in the body. They are packed with antioxidants and have anti-inflammatory properties.

Basmati Rice – is a part of the sattvic diet and balances all the doshas in the body. Rice symbolizes health and fertility in many parts of the world and is considered to be the staple food. It is easier to digest and provides nourishment to all of the tissues in the body.

As the basmati rice ages, its flavor enhances. In many eastern cultures, rice is treated with great reverence and is also used in many festivals and rituals.

Buckwheat – is a fruit seed related to rhubarb. Generally, people mistake it to be a form of wheat or a derivative of it. Buckwheat helps in balancing the vatta and Kapha doshas but increases pitta if consumed in access. It is also considered to be mildly rajasic. It is gluten-free, has low GI (Glycemic Index), and contains iron, magnesium, and protein.

Another important food item in the sattvic diet is legumes. Legumes are high in protein, complex carbohydrates, and fiber, and are low in fat content. It is believed that the smaller the legumes, the better they are.

Some of the commonly used legumes are as follows: whole mung bean, split chickpeas (also known as channa dal in India), black-eyed peas, lima beans, kidney beans, and many more. By combining whole grains with legumes we get a complete source of protein.

Fresh Organic Fruits: According to Ayurveda, fruits should be eaten when they are ripe and seasonal. Fruits that are fresh and ripe helps in digestion, provide nutrition to the body, and increase Ojas (key to perfect health and balanced emotions).

Some of the beneficial sattvic fruits according to Ayurveda:

Raw Apple – if you suffer from vatta dosha (problems like dry skin, insomnia, forgetfulness, fatigue, constipation, and many more), cooked apples and apple sauce are beneficial. Cooked apples also help build bulk, soften the stool, and relieve constipation.

Mango – is considered to be the 'king' of the ayurvedic fruits. Ripe mango is beneficial in vatta and pitta (symptoms like acid reflux, peptic ulcers, inflammation in joints, acne, loose stools, frustration, anger, and irritability) dosha. Mango also helps with constipation.

Pomegranate – has been known to be a very beneficial fruit for thousands of years. Even its part, such as the root bark, is also beneficial in many health-related conditions. It helps to balance the pitta dosha in the body. It is known to cause constipation and hence, can be used as a home remedy for diarrhea.

Bananas – are a good source of antioxidants. Ayurveda advises not to combine banana with milk or yogurt and not take any liquids within an hour of eating a banana.

Other fruits like grapes, watermelon, and pear are considered sattvic and have a lot of dosha-relieving properties.

Ayurvedic Herbs: Affiliate Disclosure: When you click links in this article and make a purchase, I get paid a small fee at no extra cost to you. This helps me run this website and produce valuable content for you. Ayurvedic herbs dated 3000 years old are said to have been used by great Indian yogis and sages, for physical and mental health benefits. Most of the eastern cultures to date use herbs to treat common problems we encounter on a day-to-day basis.

Some of the most useful herbs are as follows:

Tulsi – also known as Holi Basil is a popular ayurvedic herb that is useful in skin-related ailments, prevents blood vessel growth, strengthens the immune system, improves bone health, and much more. It balances the kapha (symptoms such as excessive mucus, white coating in the tongue, slow bowel movement, feeling foggy, dull, and lethargic) dosha and also has a pacifying effect on vatta dosha. Tulsi leaves can be chewed raw early morning or consumed with drinks such as tea and coffee.

Ashwagandha – is useful in anxiety, insomnia, stress, and adrenal dysfunction. Ashwagandha extract has the ability to lower cholesterol. It also has been said to increase sperm count in males and build stamina and endurance. When consumed early morning it keeps you activated for a longer time period in a day.

Triphala – is a combination of three Indian herbs which are haritaki, bahera, and amla. It is considered very good for digestion and is also used in the treatment of constipation. It promotes good bacteria in the gut. Triphala should be consumed in small quantities only. Too much consumption of Triphala over time may cause erosion of the gut lining.

Neem – is extremely beneficial in fungal, viral, and bacterial infections. It should always be consumed along with the food as it lowers blood sugar levels. Consuming it empty stomach can cause the blood sugar levels to go too low. People suffering from diabetes should be careful while using this herb. It also helps with the detoxification of the skin and balances excess pitta and kapha.

Although Ayurvedic herbs are generally harmless, people suffering from serious medical conditions and pregnant or nursing women should consult a certified medical professional before consuming any of these herbs.

Nuts, Seeds & Oils: Nuts are considered an important part of the diet as they are a good source of fiber, minerals, and vitamins. Oils present in the nut are a good source of fat and contain antioxidants that help fight free radicals. Nuts such as Almonds are good for energizing the mind and balancing the pitta dosha, whereas walnuts are considered astringent and are good for people with Kapha.

However, nuts should be consumed in moderation. In addition to the above, cashews and pistachio nuts offer a good source of protein.

Ayurveda believes that seeds such as pumpkin and sunflower help in pacifying the vatta dosha.

In addition, seeds like pumpkin and sunflower are also very beneficial.

According to Ayurveda, oils of almond and coconut are perfect for skin-related ailments.

On the other hand, peanuts are not considered sattvic and are generally not recommended by Ayurvedic experts, as they are difficult to digest and create lethargy in the body.

Organic Vegetables: Ayurveda suggests the use of organic vegetables for cooking without using onion and garlic which are said to be tamasic (not good for physical and mental well-being) in nature. Some of the vegetables which are considered sattvic are as follows: carrots, celery, cucumber, beets, sweet potatoes, and squash. While those that are not sattvic are mushrooms, hot peppers, and potatoes.

Ayurveda recommends drinking a juice made out of green vegetables, as it increases the prana (life-giving force) in the body.

Menu can be planned based on above parameters

CHAPTER NINE

Hyderabadi Food Festival

Food: Hyderabad are known for their unique cuisines. The city, which was once the capital for Marathis, Kannadigas, Muslims and Telugus as well, represents a unique blend of cuisines, beverages and eating habits. Dum Ka Biryani, Qubani Ka Meetha, Hyderabadi special biryani, Irani Chai, Sakinaalu, Sarva Pindi are among those specialities that others savor in Hyderabad. The hinterlands of Telangana offer a much more cuisine experience with the local flavors and spices going into the making of these dishes.

Culture: Ganga Jamuna Tehzeeb, this is how one can describe a melting pot of cultures called Hyderabad. The predominantly Muslim dominated old city, the new city inhabited by Hindus, the Secunderabad and its cantonment populated by Christians, the Parsis of Boggulkunta,Telanganas, the Sikhs, Sindhis, Marwaris, Marathis, Andhras, Tamilians, Kannadigas-everyone makes Hyderabad, as it looks today. Teeming with cultural and religious diversity, the city was considered a cosmopolitan hub even during the time of Nizam's. It is one place where one community blends into another with mutual respect and honor. Bonalu, Bathukamma, Vinayaka Chavithi and other festivals are celebrated with fervor side-by-side where the common man enjoys the festivities without any religious discrimination. The entire city lights up not just during Diwali but also Christmas. In short, Hyderabad, located almost towards the Central part of India, on the Deccan plateau represents the culmination of Urdu dialect with Telugu. The language spoken in Hyderabad is different from rest of Telangana, which is infact again categorized into various dialects for every 100-150 km. Unity in diversity, Hyderabad is a testimony to this philosophy of brotherhood and peace between various religious and cultural groups. In short, Hyderabad is a beacon of multi-religious, multi ethnic, multi cultural and multi linguistic society at peace with itself. The food, dressing habits, life style and every other aspect varies in the city which has now acquired the tag of a global city in an increasingly globalized world, where it has seamlessly blended with new ideas and people with various nationalities!

The gastronomic map of Hyderabad reflects the influence of several powerful dynasties, viz. the Qutb Shahis, the Mughals and the Nizams. The city continues to celebrate its diverse cultural identities introduced by different communities.

Music and Dance Forms of Hyderabad: The history of Hyderabad is more than 400 years old with so many cultures and traditions and vibrant and colorful mixture of dance and music which have always been famous among royal people. The most famous and important music of Hyderabad is Carnatic music. There are many popular pioneers of this music namely Muthuswamy Dikshitar, Shyama Shashtri, and Saint Tyagaraja. Hyderabad has cultural festivals for different kinds of music and dance. Thinking about the cultural dance of Hyderabad, Kuchipudi comes to the mind of everyone. It is accompanied by Carnatic music with some acting. In this form of dance, mythological tales are expressed. Another form of dance of Lord Shiva called Perini is performed in Hyderabad by a group of males only. Kathak was also introduced in the dance and poetry culture of Hyderabad.

Hyderabadi Biryani: If you were to rank the cuisine of Hyderabad by popularity, the biryani of Hyderabad will be at the top of the charts without the least confusion in the matter. Most people would be ready to consume it at any hour of the day and its rich aromatic flavour and taste never fail to bring anyone back for a second helping! It is usually made with mutton, but chicken biryani is also a hot favourite.

Haleem: Mostly made from mutton, nuts and spices and wheat, this slow-cooked dish is a hot favourite of people, without reference to religion. This dish provides special sustenance to people of Islamic faith who fast most stringently, refusing to even swallow their own saliva, for the 40 days leading up to the festival of Ramzan. Come Ramzan, everybody queues up for their fair share of this delicacy.

Hyderabadi Marag: If you always thought regular mutton soup is the only dish that soothes your palate and your soul, then you have not tried Hyderabadi Marag, Hyderabad's special soup yet. Hyderabadi Marag is a soup that is a favourite with people who like their soup spicy and with meat in it. Made of tender mutton, it is a dish fit for nawabs, as most of Hyderabad's cuisine usually is. Some restaurants serve Hyderabadi Marag with chicken meat too.

Keema Samosa: Samosas are universally popular. Know to some as Sambusas, this deep-fried item is a pastry filled with meat or vegetables, usually peas, potatoes and carrots. If on a visit to Hyderabad, be sure not to miss the Keema (Minced Mutton) Samosas available as a snack in the region. They afford a gastric sensation and satisfaction in a superior category.

Kebabs: Kebabs are a very popular barbecued meat dish, originating from Middle Eastern cuisine. Extremely popular in Hyderabad, with huge queues forming outside Hyderabadi joints for a plate of succulent, smoky kebabs and mint chutney, the meat-dish is considered a non-vegetarian's idea of paradise.

Mutton Dalcha: This uniquely Hyderabadi dish makes use of the ubiquitous mutton along with pulses and spices to tickle your palate and get you completely hooked to its taste. It's made using chickpea lentils and mutton, but can be made with vegetables too if you wish.

Kubani ka Meetha: Made of dried apricots, this is another hot favourite from Hyderabadi cuisine. This dish comes subtly flavoured and sweetened just sufficiently, and garnished with slivers of pistachios, almonds and cashew nuts. Seasoned diners order it topped with vanilla ice cream and this dessert is almost a staple at most weddings and other festivities in Hyderabad.

Double ka Meetha: This is another hot favourite item on any dessert menu in Hyderabad, including at weddings and parties. The name may seem like a misnomer, until you are told that the local slang word for bread is 'double roti' and that this sweet is basically made of fried bread, sugar syrup and garnished with slivers of nuts. You will find it served at almost every feast held on any occasion.

Irani Chai: If you are fond of tea, Irani Chai gives you a different take on that evening cup. Accompanied by a thick, sweet biscuit, Irani Chai is very milky, boiled for hours over a low flame, leaving it with a bitter, unique taste. Irani Chai is very popular in Hyderabad, with entire stalls dedicated to it. You cannot pass by an eat-street without coming across a crowd of people, tired at the end of their day, enjoying a cupful of the Irani chai and biscuits.

Sheer Korma: Sheer Korma is basically vermicelli pudding, with sweetened milk and dates. Akin to porridge, the sweet is boiled for a period, leaving it creamy and white. Usually made for festivals and functions, or just quiet afternoons, Sheer Korma is high up on the list of Indian comfort-foods. If you happen to be that sort of person, ask for dry fruits as an accompaniment, to add a crunchy note along with the nutty flavour.

Mirchi ka Salan: Even though it is a curry made entirely of chillies, the spices and flavours used make it an extremely balanced dish which does not shock your palate too much. Expect to find it quite pungent though and sour to boot. This is considered an extremely suitable side dish which goes with the ever-popular Hyderabadi biryani, along with what is called raita, or onions in curd.

Pesarattu: Pesarattu is basically a dosa – or savoury pancake – made of sprouts and lentils. It is very popular as a breakfast item in Andhra Pradesh and is usually served with ghee, chutney and upma, Pesarettu makes for a delicious breakfast, and an even better choice as a variety option at dinner. Pesarattu is high on protein and thus healthy, filling and goes very well with ginger and tamarind chutney.

Bobbatlu: Called puran poli outside South India, and Bobbatlu in Andhra Pradesh and Purnalu in Telangana, this is a form of flatbread, stuffed with a sweet filling. The filling is made of chickpeas, spices and sugar, with the bread itself made from flour and served hot with a dollop of ghee. In South India, Bobbatlu appear and taste almost like sweet chapathis, and the dessert cannot be missed in any exploration of South Indian cuisine.

Ariselu: A popular traditional South-Indian dish, used often as a dessert in festivals, parties, and events, Ariselu can brighten up the mood of even the most-exhausted wedding-goer. You will find boxes of them sitting around corner-tables especially during Sankranti, Dusshera and Deepavali. These are made of deep-fried dough, made most often of specially prepared rice flour, mixed with some form of sugar – usually jaggery, a type of cane sugar.

Pootharekulu: A thin pastry sheet made of rice – almost similar to phyllo-pastry from Greece – Pootharekulu are famous in Andhra Pradesh. They come sprinkled with sugar, pieces of cashew nuts and jaggery. Many children in South India receive boxes of this as gifts in summer – in fact, boxes of Pootharekulu exchange hands whenever relatives come visiting, or there is some form of celebration in the family. Pootharekulu is a favourite of most Telugu people, and every bite in later life is bound to come with a bout of nostalgia.

Sakinalu: Known across Andhra Pradesh and Telangana in South India as chakli or sakinalu, these are deep-fried sweetened snacks made of rice flour and black gram or chickpea flour and flavoured with sesame seeds. Made during festival time and made more enjoyable by a rainy late-afternoon or a good movie on television, these snacks beat popcorn any day. They will be found tucked in shelves in any South-Indian sweet-shop. If you happen to have a sweet tooth, ask for a packet of Gavvalu too, when you walk into that sweet shop. Thank us, later.

Maghaz Masala: Maghaz means 'brain' and masala means 'spice'. This spicy brain fry is a famous lamb dish from Hyderabad. The thick, fiery gravy with juicy meat is a must try for every non-veg lover. The best way to enjoy this traditional Hyderabadi recipe is by eating it with your hands. And don't forget to lick your fingers in the end.

Boti Kebab: Imagine hot kebabas melting in your mouth? Just the thought of this tasty preparation will give you a foodgasm. Intensely marinated mutton cooked with garden-fresh herbs is the secret behind the impeccable taste.

Khatti Dal: This piquant Hyderabadi style lentil stew will give you a loud chattka. The star ingredient of this dish is tamarind, which lends the dal its zesty flavour, making it more tempting than ever. Relish this with rice and a meat dish!

Gosht Pasinde: Weekends fly away so quickly and you still want some part of it to stay, especially the tasty lunches. Don't worry, this classical meat recipe from Hyderabad will instantly cheer you up. Just one spoonful of this thick gravy prepared with beans and potatoes is the best way to revisit your home cooked curries. We suggest you enjoy this stunning dish with hot tandoori rotis.

Malai Korma: Want to enjoy some creamy gravy? Then the palatable Malai Korma is the dish for you. The extra hint of cream gives it a rich taste. Sour tomatoes are added to balance the flavour. Serve it hot with rotis or rice.

Qabooli Biryani: This is not just any other Hyderabadi Biryani! T he vegetarian rice dish can easily give a tough competition to its non-vegetarian counterpart. It is made with nutty chana dal that provides the perfect crunch to the steaming soft biryani.

Lukhmi: Hyderabadi treat is never complete without the authentic Lukhmis. These little squares of maida filled with minced meat is just what you need to treat your taste buds. Dip it in hot chutney and savour the delectable flavour.

Hyderabadi Khichdi: If you thought khichdi is boring & bland, you're in for a pleasant surprise! Spicy in taste, the Hyderabadi khicdhi is gooey in texture and served hot with lots of desi ghee.

Kache Gosht ki Biryani: The biryani is as unique as its name. Cooked with raw meat, it is fragrant and succulent in taste. Unlike other rice recipes, the dish is a stand out main course in Hyderabad. The aroma is enough to keep you hooked but once you taste it, there is no going back. Savour it with raita to get the best out of it.

Pathar Ka Gosht: Pathar Ka Gosht is made with lamb meat. It is a famous Hyderabadi dish. It is cooked on a wide stone and put up on a flame. The spices and flavors are added to make it more delightful and flavorful. You will get here the best flavored Pathar Ka Gosht.

Hyderabadi Chicken 65: The famous and delicious Hyderabadi Chicken 65 is here to give you the best and unforgettable taste. It is served as a starter and also as a side dish. The chicken is marinated, and then it is fried. The spices are added to enhance the flavors. The best spicy and tasty Hyderabadi chicken 65 you will get here with a blast of flavor.

Baghaar-E-Baingan (Hyderabadi baingan masala): Tender aubergines/ brinjals cooked in a nutty, creamy sauce of coconut caramelised onions and peanuts. (a gravy is prepared with peanuts, tamarind, sesame seeds and brinjals cooked in it.)

Onion Kheer: With our busy schedule and changing preferences, some cuisines have become history which were otherwise very popular. One such absolutely unique dish or rather dessert was Anokhi Kheer that was made out of onions. Yes! As unusual as it may sound, this Onion Kheer was rather very common during the time of Nizams and has only disappeared 5 decades ago. Considered as a common man's dessert this Anokhi Kheer was made by combining extreme ingredients such as onions, sugar and milk which is no less a cringe worthy combination for today's generation.

Tootak was a dish, belonging to the Deccan family of recipes. The Nizams of Hyderabad would offer this dish as a welcome gesture to their guests. Well, the name itself has created such a hype that it would be unfair not to talk about what it is made of. Quite identical to modak in appearance, this appetizer cum dessert has a hard, outer shell like a short-crust pastry and a soft inside filling. The interesting bit is inside the Tootak, which is stuffed with dry fruits, milk and ghee and a meat mince. Yes, you read that right! Tootak is a one-stop shop for all kinds of flavours. These semolina pastries are then baked, even though they may appear to look deep-fried.

CHAPTER TEN

Winter Street Festival

Food travel across India is a sinful indulgence in winters. Winter is no exception to the seasonal varieties of Indian food. Indian winter delicacies including sweets and snacks are sure to leave your taste buds restless if you don't try them out. We at Indian Eagle leafed through the pages of Indian city food guides and handpicked the best delicacies that you must have in India this winter.

Gajar Ka Halwa is the most popular sweetmeat that most of the cities in the indian state offer during winter. Gajar Ka Halwa is a must on the menu of wedding feats in India.

Nolen Gurer Sandesh and Rosogolla: Kolkata treats the guests to Rosogolla and Sandesh throughout the year. But, the Bengali sweets of nolen gurer flavour (date palm jiggery) are winter specials in Kolkata. Hope, you can't afford to miss it.

Stuffed Parathas with Curd : Be it morning or evening, Delhi is fond of smoking hot Parathas in winter. Delhi specializes in serving Parathas stuffed with filling of different ingredients including spinach, cauliflower, carrot, peas, mashed potato, fenugreek leaves and reddish. Parathas with some pickle, butter and a bowl of curd give the best taste of Delhi that is unique to the North Indian food culture in winter.

Makki Ki Roti & Sarson Ka Saag : Punjab will treat you to its warm hospitality over a meal of Sarson Ka Saag and Makki Ki Roti during winter. Though this meal is cooked in the Punjabi kitchens round the year, it keeps the body warm and helps to brave the cold in Punjab during winters. The meal of Sarson Ka Saag and Makki Ki Roti is served with butter, jaggery and onion slices.

Hot Gulab Jamun with Ice-cream : Whether you are on diet or a diabetic patient, you cannot resist the temptation of hot Gulab Jamun on wintry nights. Gulab Jamun is a favourite of Indians all over the country.

Many people top Gulab Jamuns with vanilla-flavored ice-cream in winter.

Masala Khichdi with Pickle: Masala Khichdi (spicy porridge) is one of the best winter delicacies in India. It is yummy in taste and light on stomach. In winters, this traditional Indian meal is cooked with seasonal vegetables like carrots, beans, peas and cauliflower. A spoonful of ghee is the best add-on to enhance the taste.

Litti with Potato Mash or Brinjal Bharta : Winter travel to Bihar, Jharkhand and Chhattisgarh is an incomplete experience without bites of Litti Chokha. Unique to the traditional food culture of these Indian states, Littis are stuffed balls and served hot with spicy potato mash or brinjal bharta.

Samosa & Pakora with Chai: In North India, the evenings of winter are warm with platefuls of Samosa and Pakora. Stuffed with the filling of seasonal ingredients, these popular snacks are best served with cups of smoking hot tea. Samaso and Pakora with Chai are part of get-togethers and soirees in North India during winters.

Mirchi Bajji & Ragda Pattice : The spicy affair of Hyderabad begins with a plateful of Mirchi Bajji in winters. It is one of the best winter snacks and street foods in South Indian cities including Hyderabad, Chennai, Bengaluru and Mysore. It is served hot with white coconut chutney. Hyderabadis are fond of Ragda Pattice too, in the winter season.

Thukpa: Thukpa is an Indo-Tibetan noodle soup with a flavourful broth and this piping hot veggie bowl is perfect to keep you warm and cosy. It has certain variants- the Nepalese Thukpa is spicy whereas some preparations are subtle with a dash of garam masala. The noodle soup concept sits well on the palate and is a perfectly appetising bowl of comfort as food in the winter.

Gushtaba : Gushtaba is king of the Kashmiri cuisine and this winter food in India needs several steps of preparation before being served. Refusing the Gushtaba would be an insult to the host. A dish of minced mutton balls cooked in royal spices and curd, the savoury generally takes the dessert's place at a Kashmiri restaurant. Served at the end of the meal, the Gushtaba is extremely rich, heavy and perfect for the winters!

Undhiyu: Undhiyu is a dish that takes hours to make but the effort that goes into the making of it definitely pays off at the end. Mixed vegetables, fenugreek, lots of ghee and spices are what comprises of this wintery-Gujrati delicacy. Winter foods are traditionally rich and indulgent, but Undhiyu is not one of these dishes and is such a good example of healthy winter food in India.

Sakarkand Rabdi: Rabdi makes for an all-time favourite Indian dessert and Sakarkand or sweet potato rabdi is a winter speciality. It has significant nutritional contents given the generous amounts of milk, sweet potato, saffron and cardamom that go into it. Sweet potato is a perfect substitute for the health-conscious as well so wrap around your blankets and gorge on this super-sweet dish.

Gond ka Ladoo: Gond Ka Ladoo is made out of edible gum extracted from tree barks. This is one such dessert that you can eat throughout the year but can use its special nutritional powers to beat the chills of winter. The Ladoo can keep you warm since it is said to be super heaty, thus heating your insides. Once prepared, it can be kept for quite a long time, sometimes even for months.

Beetroot Thoran: A perfect accompanist to your rice meals, Beetroot Thora, is a South Indian winter speciality packed with a whole lot of nutrition and flavour. Thoran is cooked with chillies and Haldi, and the beetroot is stir-fried along with the spices to complete the dish. It is said to be a winter dish because it has a perfect blend of sweet and spicy, which is just the remedy for the chills!

Nihari: Nihari is a dish cooked with beef, mutton or chicken and is a soup curry usually consumed for breakfast. This spicy winter food is prepared overnight and had with puris, makes for a hearty indulgent breakfast. The dish takes all night to cook until the meat turns soft and tender, which swiftly melts in the mouth. With hours of effort dedicated to the dish, the delicacy is simply irresistible. You can afford to eat such an indulgent meal only on a crisp winter morning.

Lapsi : Lapsi is a breakfast sweet consumed especially in Gujarat and parts of Rajasthan. There are certain variants of lapsi available in different parts of the country. A generous amount of ghee, dry fruits, broken wheat, and raisins are put into the dish. It is a great breakfast delicacy to keep warm throughout the day.

Til Pitha: Til pitha is an Assamese sweet dish. It's a kind of pancake stuffed with sesame seeds and jaggery. Since the best of jaggery is found in winters, til pitha is best prepared and served as a winter food in India too. It's a combination of soft and crunchy and is relished at any time of the day.

Carrot Poriyal: Carrot Poriyal is a South Indian spin to the beans Poriyal dish. Extremely delicious, fresh carrot goes into the making. Carrots are stir-fried with a whole lot of spices mixed with some chilly paste, cumin seeds, and freshly grated coconut. The sweetness from the carrots and the spice from the chillies gives it a perfect balance and makes for a good side dish with any Indian meal.

Chikki: The Indian nutritious bar of nuts and jaggery is a perfect crispy dessert. You can ditch your chocolates for this healthy sweet substitute. It serves as a snack, a good dessert or just something to munch on while you beat your boredom. A chikki a day is sure to keep the winter chills away!

Raab: Another winter drink, raab is a chilli beverage balanced with the right amount of millet flour and sweet. Raab is great to boost immunity. You can definitely get the chilly-hit on the first sip itself! However, this traditional Gujrati and Rajasthan drink just can't be put down at one sip.

Panjiri: Panjiri is a delicious wheat mixture of ghee, sugar, and lots of almonds. You can keep eating it without realising the amount you've gorged on. The goodness of ghee and nuts will keep you fit and glowing during the winters, so why just stop at one serving?

Paya Shorba: A mutton soup dish, Paya Shorba is a non-vegetarians winter delight! Aromatic and flavourful spices added with lamb trotters in the soup is just a heart-warming dish. It's super easy to prepare and also makes for the perfect bowl of hot soup and is a favourite winter food in India.

Methi Pakora: With the availability of the best methi produce in winters, seizing the opportunity of eating pakoras with a hot cup of Chai is very important. Methi pakoras are irresistible, and there isn't any limit to eating them. You need to eat to your heart's content until next winter.

Malai Makhan: Malai Makhan, also known as Khimish or Daulat ki Chaat is a seasonal beverage available between October and March. Rich in preparation, lighter in taste, this drink is made by churning milk and cream until it evolves into a feathery-froth. It is finally embellished with dry fruits, khoya, or saffron. It makes for a great early morning winter drink with a hearty breakfast.

So now you know what winter food in India to keep you warm and fuzzy. Don't miss out on the opportunity to eat as many winter dishes you can so that you don't have to wait until the next season.

Misal Pav: Hailing from Maharashtra, misal pav is one of the spiciest street foods in the country, and is adored by many in the nation. Made with moth bean sprouts and a melange of flavours, this road delicacy is garnished off with chivda, sev, coriander, green chilli.

Momo: Well, this needs no introduction. Indians are fond of momos, served hot with a spicy sauce and soup. It's great to have during winters undoubtedly! You can get them anywhere, all around the country. But if you really want to taste in its truest sense, pay a visit to a north-eastern state!

Habshi Halwa is a milk halwa that is made by curdling, sweetening and flavoring milk. It is a slightly tedious task to cook the halwa as it takes long to get it to the right consistency. But it is worth the effort because it brings together the best of milk solids, ghee and nuts, into a right Indian dessert.

Shakarkandi Ki Chaat: Shakarkandi chaat is a sweet and tangy street snack made of sweet potatoes (shakarkandi) seasoned with chaat masala, spices, and aromatics, and served with a variety of toppings. In Delhi, where the original shakarkandi chaat dish was developed, street food sellers sell it from their thelas (handcarts). Shakarkandi roasted over a charcoal fire has a seductive smokey flavour and scent. Shakarkandi chaat is not only a delicious snack, but it is also a favourite cuisine during fasting times for Hindu holidays such as Navratri, Mahashivratri, and Ekdashi. It is eaten on upwas or vrat (fasting) days because it is full, healthy, and delicious.

Skyu: a traditional soup-like Ladakhi delicacy made with veggies and wheat dough kneaded into flat thumb-size balls, is one of the lesser-known winter specialties. These flat balls are cooked on low heat with water and root vegetables like carrots and turnips and served with meat. This is a staple in the region to beat the cold temperatures that frequently fall below freezing during the winter. Skyu is also available in oma (milk) form, which substitutes milk for water as the main ingredient.

Jhola nolen gur: the crown gem of Bengal's sweet delights, is the freshest batch of liquid date palm jaggery with a rich sweet texture with woody and caramel overtones. It comes in two types: liquid and solid. The liquid version is known as Jhole nolen gur, while the solid version is known as Patali gur. While both can be consumed on their own without any accompaniment, they are also used to make a variety of desserts such as Pithe, Sandesh, and Payesh. Nolen gurer roshogolla and payesh is a must-order dessert.

Chi Al Meh: Most of us have had our fill of Thukpas, but this northern delicacy is a flavor-packed bomb that will keep all winter cold at bay. This delightful broth stew is a traditional Manipuri cuisine cooked with veggies like onions, capsicum, mushrooms, spinach, and a lot of ginger, chillies, and other ingredients. Chi Al Meh is typically eaten as a nutritious dish on its own, but it can also be coupled with noodles.

Zan : Zan of Arunachal Pradesh is a famous porridge recipe in Arunachal Pradesh. It is simple to prepare and tasty to eat. This tasty spicy porridge provides a flavour roller coaster and is ideal for cold winter days. While enjoying the warmth of Zan this winter, one can be assured of good taste and nourishment.

Chholia Pulav : Fresh green peas are plentiful during the New Year basant. Green chickpeas, also known as chholia or hare chaney, are a desi favourite that can be found in vegetarian and meat curries, as well as a variety of traditional dishes such as chholia pulav (spiced vegetable rice dish containing cooked chholia). When combined with plain rice, it creates a refreshing twist on classic pulao. It's a basic dish that's great for quick preparation, especially when you're looking for light dinners.

Tilkut From Bihar: Immensely popular in the state of Bihar, Tilkut is a traditional sweet, especially made and eaten during the festival of Makar Sankranti. Also known as Til Kuta and Tilkatri, this sweet is made of grounded till or what is more popularly known as sesame seeds, coupled with generous amounts of gud or jaggery. Traditionally, the sesame seeds are pounded by hand, and made into a disc-like shape, although circular, oval, cylindrical, or even cuboid shapes are common as well.

Bafauri From Chattisgarh: An unassuming, no-frills snack popular in the state of Chattisgarh, you can think of Bafauri as a healthier alternative to your general pakodas. The primary ingredient in this light dish is that of steamed Chana Dal, with seasonal vegetables getting added to the mix in some recipes, for a healthier and more filling version.

CHAPTER ELEVEN

Turkish Food Festival

Turkish cuisine is one of the most appetizing and rich cuisines of the world, and Turkish people are known to be quite passionate about food. Diversity and the full flavor makes the Turkish cuisine worldwide famous which draws influences from its rich history and each region in the country today praises its own specialities. The richness of Turkish cuisine is based on several factors: Variety of products cultivated on the lands of Asia and Anatolia, numerous cultural interactions in history, the palace kitchens of Seljuk and Ottoman empires and geographical conditions that shaped the character of Turkish culinary culture. The Turkish art of cooking has a long and deep-rooted past and its cuisine varies across the country. The culinary culture of Istanbul, Bursa, Izmir region inherits many elements of vast Ottoman cuisine. The Marmara, Aegean and Mediterranean cuisines are rich in vegetables, fresh herbs and fish. Olive oil is most widely used. Black Sea region's cuisine uses fish extensively, especially the Black Sea anchovy (hamsi). It's influenced by Balkan and Slavic cuisine and includes maize dishes. The cuisine of the southeast—Urfa, Gaziantep and Adana—is famous for its kebabs and dough-based desserts such as baklava, kadayıf and künefe. Central Anatolia has it's own specialties, such as keşkek, mantı and gözleme.

An overview of the Turkish food varieties;

- Çorbalar: Soups, generally served before the main dish, especially in winter season.
- Mezeler: Mezes, Mostly cold served, olive oil based appetizers.
- Dolma & Sarma: Stuffed vegetables or rolled leaves with rice or meat stuffings.
- Salatalar: Salads of various kinds from different regions.
- Zeytinyağlılar: Olive oil vegetable dishes which are usually served cold.

- Pilavlar: Rice or bulgur pilaf variations.
- Etliler: Meat dishes mostly cooked with vegetables.
- Börekler: Stuffed or rolled pastries with meat, cheese or vegetable fillings.
- Pideler: Kind of flat bread with cheese, vegetables or meat.
- Kebaplar: Kebabs range from kebabs cooked in a pot to skewered kebabs.
- Balık ve Deniz Ürünleri: Fish and other seafood such as shrimps and squids.
- Tatlılar: Desserts that range from milk-based tastes to baklava like pastries.

The Key Ingredients of Turkish Cuisine

The core of Turkey's culinary marvels consists of a wide variety of ingredients. Generally, Turkish cuisine consists of vegetables, legumes, meats, spices, grains, nuts, and oils.

- Nuts typically consist of chestnuts, almonds, walnuts, hazelnuts, and pistachios.
- Legumes include chickpeas, lentils, beans, and broad beans.
- Meats usually include lamb, chicken, beef, and fish.
- Rice and bulgur are widely used as grains. Traditional Turkish oils include olive oil, sunflower oil, and hazelnut oil.
- There is a whole spectrum of spices, including red pepper, thyme, mint, coriander, black pepper, saffron, nigella seeds, rosemary, coriander, cumin, sumac, poppy seeds, and cloves.
- There are also a whole lot of vegetables. These include okra, pea, zucchini, chicory, carrot, green peppers, spinach, artichoke, tomato, mallow, cabbage, celery, potatoes, cauliflower, mushrooms, asparagus, beets, leek, lettuce, arugula, eggplant, purslane, radish, and garlic to name a few.

Popular vegetable ingredients/dishes in the Turkish menu include:

- Kizartma: Deep-fried vegetables like potatoes, zucchini, green peppers, and eggplant. They are usually served with a yogurt source.
- Mucver: Graded vegetables mixed with flour and egg before being deep-fried. The most common ingredient is zucchini.

- Karniyarik: Eggplant stuffed with chopped-up garlic, green peppers, onions, tomatoes, and ground beef and baked in an oven.
- Kabak oturtma: Zucchini roasted with minced beef or lamb.
- Kapuska: Thin white cabbage stiffed with onions and tomato sauce. It can also be cooked with minced lamb or beef.
- Turlu: Prepared by cooking zucchini, onions, potatoes, eggplant, and onion.
- Ispanak yemegi: Spinach, onions, and rice cooked with tomato paste and eaten with garlic yogurt.

Some popular types of bread in Turkey include:

- Somun Ekmek: This bread has a soft golden yellow color and is one of the most consumed in Anatolia.
- Lavas: Lavas bread is commonly used to make wraps. It is prepared from water, flour, and salt.
- Pide: Also known as pita, pide bread is a type of flatbread.
- Misir Ekmegi: This bread is prepared from cornflour and is high in nutrients. It is common in the Eastern Black Sea Region.
- Yufka Ekmek: This wheat bread has been consumed in Anatolia for thousands of years. When fresh, it is the main ingredient in pancakes and borek. On the other hand, it can be made to last for up to 12 months if fried up.

Manti is another wheat-based cuisine in Turkey. This dish consists of dough dumplings filled with a special meat mix. Its usually taken during the weekends as lunch and is served with a dash of melted butter and garlic yogurt as accompaniments.

Borek is another popular wheat-based meal. The dish consists of thin sheets of dough layered or folded into various shapes and filled with meat mixes or cheese. These are either baked or fried before being served.

Soups

There are more than 200 soup recipes in Turkey, making the Turkish soup menu the richest and most diverse globally. You can practically have soup for breakfast, lunch, and supper if you want to. Some common soups in the country include:

- Cold ayranasi soup, prepared from bulgur and chickpeas. It's a tasty and nutritious soup commonly consumed in the summer and can be served chilled or lukewarm.
- Lentil soup (mercimek corbasi), prepared from red lentils, potatoes, and lamb/chicken stock and spiced with carrots, onions, and garlic.
- Chicken and vermicelli soup (Sehriyeli tavuklu corbasi), prepared from chicken, vermicelli, and butter.
- Tomato soup (Domates Corbasi), a roasted tomato soup that served as a prelude to most Turkish lunches and dinners. Ingredients include tomatoes, garlic, onion, olive oil, flour, water, fresh basil leaves, salt, and freshly ground black pepper.

Others include tripe soup (iskembe torbasi), tarhana soup (tarhana corbasi), and cheek and shank soup (kellepaca corbasi).

Meat

Those who love meat will find a home and a full stomach in Turkish cuisine. The country has some of the sweetest and most iconic meat dishes globally, like kofte and kebab. Meat comes from chicken, beef, and lamb and is prepared in various methods; roasted, grilled, fried, skewered, etc.

Kebabs are perhaps the biggest export of Turkish meat cuisine. In Turkey, it's cooked both at home and in restaurants using spiced beef, lamb, or chicken. . Every region in Turkey has its unique kebab style.

The western world is more familiar with the doner and sis kebab varieties. Doner is prepared by stacking alternating layers of sliced lamb leg and ground meat on a large skewer. The vertical skewer is slowly rotated to roast the outer layer of the meat, from which thin slices will be shaved to be served. On the other hand, sis kebab is grilled cubes of skewered meat.

There are other kebab variants, which are cooked in pots drily without water. These are easier to prepare than grilled kebabs and, thus, commonly prepared at home.

Kofte can be prepared using ground beef or lamb, skewered meats, or grilled meats and grilled tomatoes, eggplant, and peppers. It is a common delicacy in family picnics.

Nomadic Turks inspired raw kofte. It is prepared by kneading raw double ground meat with thing bulgur and hot spices for several hours.

Izgara refers to the general way used to prepare meat dishes in Turkish meat restaurants. These include kofte, shish, or lamb chops. In Turkey, you'll find two types of restaurants; those specializing in only grilled meats (meat restaurants) and those selling meat alongside other local dishes.

Fish & Seafood

Bathed by four seas, the Mediterranean, Aegean, Marmara, and the Black Sea, Turkey is rich in fish and seafood. However, to get a good taste of these, you must visit the coastal areas because fish and seafood in the interior are pretty expensive.

Fish in Turkey is prepared by frying, grilling, or cooking slowly by the poaching (bugulama) method. The most popular fish in Turkish cuisine is the anchovies, which are usually served cornflour-coated. They can also be prepared in a variety of ways, but their availability depends on the season.

Typical fish dishes include mackerel, sardines, bonito, farmed sea bass, and farmed sea bream. Seafood, on the other hand, is mainly served in restaurants. These include clams, oysters, crabs, octopuses, bugs, lobsters, prawns, calamari, scallops, and squid.

Turkish Street Food

Turkey is home to some of the best street foods in the world. These are quickly prepared, delicious, and thus, a firm favorite among locals and tourists. Some of the most famous street foods in the country include Doner, Pide, Gozleme, Lahmacun, Simit, kofte ekmek, cig kofte, Kokorec, and Kumpir.

Doner: Doner is an old Turkish favorite that has also become a famous dish in a lot of Western countries. A compressed lamb and beef combination is grilled slowly as it spins on a vertical rotisserie by an open flame. As it rotates, the cone of doner meat is roasted by the flame and then slowly carved down in very thin slices with a very long knife. The meat is then served on bread or lavas wrap (durum) with your choice of tasty tomatoes, onions, lettuce, yogurt, and potatoes.

Gozleme: Known as the Turkish pancake, gozleme is a simple traditional Turkish food, however, it is often listed among the specialties at certain small eating spots. A very thin sheet of dough, similar to a crepe, is baked on a curved sheet of metal and then filled with cheese, potato, spinach, or ground meat, and is always served fresh.

Pide: Most commonly referred to as a Turkish 'pizza' because this fast food is made with thick dough and topped with a selection of meats, vegetables, and cheeses. Made fresh to order in a wood-fired oven, pide is usually long and oval-shaped as and cut into many slices to enjoy.

Lahmacun: This delicious Turkish version of pizza is made from a thin layer of pastry on which minced meat is spread with tomato, onion, salt, and parsley, and spiced with red pepper to your liking. Generally, Turks fill the center with tomatoes, lettuce, and onions and a sprinkle of lemon juice, and roll to eat.

Further reading: The Best Lahmacun in Istanbul: 6 Outstanding Lahmacun Places

One of the simple pleasures of Turkish cuisine is a ring-shaped bread covered by sesame seeds. Simit can be found easily everywhere in Turkey, and most commonly sold on the streets, displayed in small covered carts or small stands, and sometimes simply carried by a walking vendor with simit piled high on his head. The simit looks like a plain bread roll but is a favorite breakfast accompaniment, or snack on the streets of Istanbul, usually enjoyed with some cheese and ayran.

Kokorec: One of the favorite fast foods of Turks, this dish made from sheep intestines is flavored with herbs and served in bread tomatoes, onions and parsley. Despite how it sounds, it's actually delicious and you can find the best kokorec in Kadikoy, Ortakoy and Balik Pazari districts of Istanbul.

Kumpir: This Turkish food is simply made from large baked potatoes which are then cut in half and filled with your choice of a variety of fillings, including cheese, olives, salads, pickles, peas, mushrooms, sausages, and corn.

Kofte ekmek: One of the best street foods you will find, usually sold from minivans. The bread is filled with kofte (meatballs) and onion, hot spices, tomato, salad, and parsley.

Cig kofte: This fantastically simple and healthy food is enjoyed in the streets all over Istanbul. Meaning 'raw meatballs' the most common varieties now are made without meat and are a raw bulgur meatball 'cooked' in spices. Cig kofte is generally served wrapped in a lettuce leaf and sprinkled with fresh lemon juice.

Turkish Beverages

Turkish tea: Turks love tea, and most Turks drink many cups a day. Turkish tea is always offered first to visitors and guests to all homes and businesses. Turks prepare tea by brewing it in a teapot (not with 'tea bags'), preferably porcelain, over a kettle, and a perfectly brewed Turkish tea should be a deep red color. Although tea can be found served in porcelain cups at the major hotels and cafes, Turks prefer to have their tea served in glass cups. Although instant coffee (which Turks call 'Nescafe') is quite common, nothing can take the place of a good cup of tea. Tea gardens (cay bahcesi) abound in Istanbul. These open-air gardens, usually located in areas with stunning panoramic views, also serve fruit juice, colas, and some Turkish food like sandwiches and 'tost' (grilled sandwiches). More traditional tea gardens serve their tea with a semaver (a metal teapot), and in some tea gardens, you'll even find nargile (water pipe) for smoking an array of fruit-flavored tobacco. The tea gardens of Moda and Emirgan are popular choices among café-goers.

Turkish coffee: Turkish coffee is served in small porcelain cups (resembling espresso cups) and always with a glass of water. It is not usually consumed with breakfast; but, more commonly, it is enjoyed after meals with something sweet, usually Turkish delight or chocolate. Turkish coffee is traditionally prepared in a small copper pot called a cezve, and is made by boiling an extremely finely ground coffee together with water and sugar. The coffee is served according to your taste – sade (without sugar) or sekerli (sweet). While drinking you should sip the coffee lightly, to leave the coffee grounds at the bottom of the cup.

Ayran: This delicious drink made from yogurt diluted with water and then salted and served cold is very much enjoyed by Turks and is the perfect accompaniment to most meals, especially kebab or spicy Turkish foods.

Sahlep: This hot drink usually enjoyed on cold winter days is made from the dried powdered roots of a mountain orchid. Sahlep powder is mixed with milk and sugar and boiled. The roots are rich in starch and the mixture thickens naturally, resembling a cream-like texture. It is generally served plain and sprinkled with cinnamon, but you can also find it as a milk replacement for lattes and other coffees during winter.

Turnip juice: A sour, sometimes hot, crimson-colored drink prepared by boiling turnips and carrots in water, and adding vinegar. Originating in Southern Anatolia, it can relieve an upset stomach, helps the body to cope with the heat, and is also one of the more preferred accompaniments of some spicy Turkish food like kebab, cigkofte, and raki.

Boza: This thick, slightly sour drink is made from crushed millet and water, which has been left to ferment. Boza is most commonly enjoyed in winter, and Boza houses serve glasses of the drink decorated with cinnamon or chickpeas.

Raki: This is probably the most well-known of all Turkey's alcoholic drinks – and certainly one of the most enjoyed food accompaniments among Turks. This aniseed-flavored drink contains high degree of alcohol and should not be consumed quickly. Rather, most people enjoy the colorless raki mixed with water, which turns it into a cloudy-white drink.

Raki is widely said to aid digestion and is known as a kind of aperitif.

Alcoholic drinks, on the other hand, are pretty appreciated, despite the country being considered to be predominantly Muslim. Raki is a famous traditional Turkish alcoholic drink that contains a high alcohol percentage and thus, should be consumed slowly. Here is a detailed read on how to drink Raki aka the lion's milk.

Few Classic dishes

1. Baklava: Dating back to the Ottoman Empire, baklava is one of the most iconic Turkish dishes and a must for anyone with a sweet tooth. This layered pastry is filled with nuts and covered in syrup and ground pistachios for an unforgettable Mediterranean dessert. You can find baklava in most bakeries and supermarkets, but it's best when freshly baked.

2. Şiş kebap: 'Kebab' is an umbrella term that encompasses a variety of street eats, but the most famous is the skewered şiş kebap. Traditionally made of beef or lamb, today diners can choose from a wider selection of meat, fish, poultry and vegetarian options, grilled over charcoal and served on metal or wooden skewers.

3. Döner: The other famous kebab, the döner offers the same diversity in the choice of meat, which is seasoned with herbs and spices and cooked on a vertical, rotating spit. Fresh cuts are served in a bread wrap along with salad and garlic or spicy sauces.

4. Köfte: Turkish 'meatballs' come in all shapes and sizes, and can be eaten solo as street snacks, dipped in plain yoghurt or served with rice and salad. Different regions of Turkey have christened their own distinctive varieties, including Izgara Köfte, served with grilled peppers, rice and bread, and Çiğ Köfte, eaten raw.

5. Pide: Commonly known as 'Turkish pizza,' like its Italian cousin, pide is a flat pastry base topped with cheese and assorted meat and vegetables, heated in a stone oven. The choice of toppings is practically limitless, making pide and its leaner counterpart lahmacun ideal for vegetarians and diners with other dietary requirements.

6. Kumpir: A cheap and flexible street food staple in Istanbul's bustling Ortaköy district, kumpir is a crispy baked potato with your choice of creative fillings.

7. Meze: If you're having trouble choosing from the menu, get a crash course in a range of traditional delicacies with these cold appetisers. A typical meze includes about 20 items, from bean dishes and salads to dips and spreads, served with bread and drinks.

8. Dolma: Vegetarian Delicacy: Fresh vegetables or dried eggplants, peppers, tomatoes or zucchinis are stuffed with a mixture of rice and onion before cooking in water and butter. These are usually served at room temperature. It is a popular Mediterranean cuisine and is found in regions beyond Turkey. It is believed that this dish was originated in the Ottoman Topkapi Palace back in the 17th century.

9. Yaprak Sarma: A Healthy Snack: Vine leaves wrapped around a filling of rice and onion flavored with mint, currant, pepper and cinnamon are steamed to prepare what is an exquisitely healthy Yaprak Sarma. It is a traditional food in Turkey that is packed with enormous amount of flavors. This dish has an influence of ottoman Empire, and is famous from Middle East to South Eastern Europe. The preparation of this dish is a bit time-consuming but it is all worth it.

10. Kunefe:If you have a sweet tooth, then Kunefe is a special food in Turkey that all dessert-lovers must try on their vacation. The delightful dessert is made with cheese, bread crumbs, and pistachio nuts. The dessert is so delicious and sinful that you won't be able to stop yourself from having a single serving.

11. Halva: The Turkish halva is made from tahini (crushed sesame paste) and sugar, sometimes with other ingredients added. This is nothing like what you have in India apart the name it shares, and that's what makes it one of the most distinguished Turkish foods. It tastes way different than over conventional halva dish and the method of preparation is entirely different. You have got to try this on your vacation in Turkey.

CHAPTER TWELVE

Greek Food Festival

Greek cuisine has a culinary tradition of some 4,000 years and is a part of the history and the culture of Greece. Its flavors change with the season and its geography.Greek cookery, historically a forerunner of Western cuisine, spread its culinary influence - via ancient Rome - throughout Europe and beyond.Many well-known Greek dishes are in fact part of the larger tradition of the food of the Ottoman Empire, with classic dishes such as moussaka,yuvarlakia, keftethes, boureki and tzatziki having Arabic, Persian and Turkish roots.It has influences from the different people's cuisine the Greeks have interacted with over the centuries, as evidenced by several types of sweets and cooked foods.

It was Archestratos in 320 B.C. who wrote the first cookbook in history.

From some of the best lamb dishes on earth to fresh seafood, vegetables, beans, pulses and, of course, good olive oil, Greek food is simple, colourful and incredibly nutritious. Like other Mediterranean cuisines, Greek food has a reputation for being heart healthy with its heavy use of olive oil, fish, lean meats, vegetables, herbs and grain, although some dishes can be quite rich, like the classic moussaka – a hearty dish made of layers of lamb and eggplant, smothered in béchamel sauce and cheese.

Greek cuisine uses some flavorings more often than other Mediterranean cuisines do, namely: oregano, mint, garlic, onion,dill and bay laurel leaves. Other common herbs and spices include basil, thyme and fennel seed. Parsley is also used as a garnish on some dishes. Many Greek recipes, especially in the northern parts of the country, use "sweet" spices in combination with meat, for example cinnamon, whole spice and cloves in stews.

Some dishes can be traced back to ancient Greece: lentil soup, fasolada and pasteli (candy bar with sesame seeds baked with honey) some to the Hellenistic and Roman periods: loukaniko (dried pork sausage) and

Byzantium: feta cheese, avgotaraho (cured fish roe) and paximadi (traditional hard bread baked from corn, barley and rye). There are also many ancient and Byzantine dishes which are no longer consumed: porridge as the main staple, fish sauce, and salt water mixed into wine.

Mezes refers to small dishes, which frequently help make up a main meal, served with salads, dips and pita bread. Besides the ever-present olive oil, other widely used ingredients and flavorings include eggplant, tomatoes, potato, okra, lemon, cheese, herbs and honey. Greece's climate favors the breeding of sheep, making beef dishes less common in traditional fare. Many dishes are wrapped in filo pastry - including Greek classics such as spanakopita (spinach and feta) and the honey-drenched, nut filled dessert baklava. As for beverages, strong Greek coffee, retsina (white wine with pine resin added),raki,tsipouro and the 80-percent-proof anise flavoured ouzo are all ever popular.

When Greeks taste something delicious, they have a lovely phrase "Yia Sta Heria Sas" which translates as "Your hands are blessed", celebrating the skill of the cook.

Greek Ingredients

The traditional Greek diet is based around vegetables and fruits, wholegrains, beans and legumes, fish, and some dairy like cheese and yoghurt. Because of the climate, Greece is rich with an array of fruits and vegetables, and many Greeks work in or adjacent to agriculture (or at least grow lots of food in their own gardens) - so utilising good quality raw ingredients is a no-brainer. Alongside the Greek propensity to cover everything in olive oil (a healthy fat), Greek and Mediterranean Diets are regarded as some of the healthiest in the world.

Apricot, peach, nectarine and cherry trees grow easily, amongst the later figs and grapes scattering hillsides. Melon and watermelon especially are favourite summertime desserts, whilst in winter we enjoy the bounty of citrus fruits like mandarins, oranges and lemons, as well as kiwis. The warm days encourage tomatoes, aubergines and peppers, alongside a full roster of vegetables from peas to potatoes to beans, and plentiful herbs. Olive trees, of course, are central to the cuisine. Alongside the olive oil is feta cheese - not grown, but made, from sheep's milk. Greek olive oil and Greek feta are absolutely foundational, and very few Greeks are prepared to substitute these - these two ingredients are the heart of many a traditional recipe!

Baked moussaka: The most famous of Greek dishes, moussaka consists of layers of fried aubergine, minced meat and potatoes. That's all topped with a creamy béchamel sauce and then baked until golden brown. you can also serve an equally delectable vegetarian version.

Fasolatha : Is this classic white bean soup. It's a simple, yet hearty affair consisting of beans, crushed tomatoes, and vegetables such as onions, carrots and celery. It's often flavoured with thyme, parsley and bay leaves.

Sesame-covered koulouri: Walk around any of the big Greek cities such as Athens or Thessaloniki in the mornings and you'll often see locals on their way to work munching on koulouri – large soft bread rings covered in sesame seeds.

Stuffed yemista: Is made of juicy local vegetables, typically tomatoes or peppers, that are stuffed with rice and then roasted in the oven. Some versions of Yemista (which in Greek means 'filled with') also include minced meat.

Loukoumades: Small fried doughnut-like balls drenched in honey syrup and sprinkled with various toppings such as cinnamon or crushed walnuts. People usually order a large plate of them to share with friends or family. This is Greek dining at its very best.

Grill souvlaki: Grilled meat (usually pork) skewers are often served hot off of the grill. Typically one enjoys souvlaki with tzatziki, pita bread, salad, tomato or rice. The Athen's version of this dish, kalamaki, is usually marinated overnight.

Stuffed grape leaves or dolmades: Dolmades are a typical greek side dish. They are made of vine or grape leaves stuffed with herby, lemony rice and folded over to create a small parcel, which is then steamed. You can also find them filled with meat or vegetarian with rice only.

Meatball — keftethes: Keftethes are essentially Greek breaded meatballs — typically made with lamb meat and grated potatoes and served with a creamy yoghurt sauce. They are crispy, juicy, and can be enjoyed with salad or rice on the side. This is a classic Greek food to try when visiting.

Cheese pie — spanakopita: The Greeks love their pies and you can find many varieties, from those made with enriched dough to those made from flaky phyllo (also filo) pastry and filled with anything from aubergines or meat to greens or cheese. The most classic is the spanakopita – phyllo pastry layered with feta cheese and spinach and flavoured with dill. Another favourite is tyropita – crunchy phyllo pastry wrapped around a savoury cheese filling.

Stifado: Stifado is an understated Greek meat stew, perfect for colder months. It is typically made with beef or rabbit, tomatoes and often small whole onions. Typically stewed for hours, this traditional greek comfort food is a great dish to try on your trip.

Gyros : A bit like a kebab, a gyro is a typical Greek sandwich. It consists of pieces of meat (usually chicken, pork, lamb or beef) cooked on a rotisserie and wrapped in a flatbread or pita along with salad, onions and a variety of sauces. Vegetarian versions can include grilled halloumi (a salty Cypriot cheese made from a mix of sheep's and goat's milk) or feta cheese instead of the meat.

Galaktoboureko: These sweet custard slices, made with layers of flaky phyllo pastry and sprinkled with cinnamon, are worth a visit to Greece alone, even if you don't do anything else.

Papoutsakia: The word "Papoutsakia" in Greek means "little shoes". This dish consists of eggplants scooped out and stuffed with eggs, bell peppers, minced meat, tomatoes, lemon and olive oil. This hearty dish is then topped with local salty cheeses.

Baklava — a true classic: Found all over Greece, Turkey and the Middle East, baklavas are small sweet pastries soaked in honey-like syrup and layered with crushed nuts such as walnuts or almonds. In central Greece, they are made with almonds, in the eastern regions with walnuts and in northern Greece with pistachios.

Choriatiki: A trip to Greece is not complete without trying Choriatiki or greek salad. Feta cheese sits on top of fresh vegetables — cucumbers, juicy tomatoes, bell peppers, and sliced red onion — then is sprinkled in greek olives and extra virgin olive oil. This simple but truly iconic dish is a perfect way to start a meal, especially on a hot day.

Kleftiko: This classic rustic dish is a combination of lamb, potatoes and tomatoes that are sealed in a piece of parchment paper and cooked together for hours. Traditionally, this dish was cooked in a fire pit buried underground — which is why it is called Kleftiko or "hidden meat". Made with simple local and flavourful ingredients, Kleftiko is a perfect example of traditional Greek food at its best.

Pastitsio : Similar to Italian lasagne, but made with small macaroni instead of pasta sheets, this is Greek comfort food at its best. Greek cuisine has long been influenced by Italy, particularly in the Kefalonia area. Pastitsio is made by layering ground beef or lamb with macaroni and béchamel sauce and is often flavoured with cinnamon, nutmeg and Greek herbs. Sometimes it's also topped with grated cheese before being baked in the oven.

Amygdalota: These crunchy and chewy almond cookies are sometimes referred to as "Greek Macaroons". They are typically sweetened with orange blossoms or rose water and pair perfectly with a cup of coffee in the afternoon.

Giouvetsi: Giouvesti (sometimes spelled yiouvetsi, youvetsi, or yuvetsi) is a baked dish made with kritharaki pasta (similar in some ways to orzo). The pasta stews together with either lamb meat or seafood in a clay pot, and cheese is added right before serving.

Tzatziki: Made with a greek yoghurt and cucumber base, this dish is great as an appetiser or mezédhes and is eaten usually with bread or fried eggplant. It is also enjoyed as a sauce to accompany other dishes. Tzatziki has tangy flavours of lemon and dill and its tradition in Greece dates back to before the Ottoman empire.

Soutzoukakia: A classic Greek food, soutzoukakia are oblong greek meatballs served in a somewhat spicy tomato sauce with cumin. In some parts of Greece, this dish is served on top of square-shaped egg pasta. In others, served on rice.

Retsina: Some of the most admired wines in antiquity were produced in Greece. Retsina wine is a white wine that has been made in Greece for thousands of years. The name translates to 'resinated' and gets its distinctive flavour due to its contact with Aleppo pine resin.

CHAPTER THIRTEEN

Italian Food Festival

The Italian culture has a very rich tradition in food, arts, music, literature. The list goes on. Italian food is considered one of the best food palates in the world. It is full of flavor that will surely tantalize your taste buds which you will surely enjoy. If you are wondering about all of the buzzes with the Italian food culture you should know everything about this amazing food. If you are very pleased with the flavors of Italian food you would surely love it more if you better understand its entire concept.

The Italian peninsula is packed with diverse culinary cultures which produce different Italian dishes. For instance, Sicily produces seafood dishes while Tuscany is best known for its simple yet rustic specials.

Other nationalities from different countries have also adopted the Italian food tradition and have even become a staple food on their tables. For example, Americans are very much in love with pizza and pasta which is a popular Italian dish. Additionally, Italian food culture uses distinct ingredients for all of their dishes such as tomato, eggplant, pasta, cured meats, and cheese. You must not forget about the sweet Italian desserts that will surely conclude your meal with a bang.

Italian food culture has influenced a lot of countries already. It is known to captivate the taste buds of so many people from different cultures around the world. Thus, these people adopted what they liked about Italian food and added locally grown ingredients and incorporated them into their own traditional dishes, and made them their own. The most important aspect that you must know about the Italian food culture is that their authentic dishes are only made with a few ingredients. However, these ingredients are carefully chosen and if the ingredient is not the freshest it can be they will not buy it but substitute for better quality or not make the dish at all. Each ingredient must shine since there are only a few ingredients.

All Fresh Ingredients: The ingredients used in cooking are nothing but fresh. The Italian food culture focuses more on choosing fresh, quality ingredients than on intricate preparations. Italy is a pretty diverse country and every region offers different fresh produce that makes it readily available throughout Italy. From fresh eggs to oil, vegetables, meat, fish, herbs, and cheeses, Italian food is all about the freshness of all the ingredients they put into their dishes.

Tradition: Italy has a rich tradition. Each region boasted its own dishes where they carefully incorporated their respective traditions. Contrary to what most people from other parts of the world might have thought, no place in Italy eats the same dish as the next.

In the north of Italy, for instance, people in this region cook more meat, potatoes, and rice than their neighboring areas. The very popular Italian dishes like pizza and pasta are more local in the central part of Italy. While in the South, their dishes are usually cooked with fresh tomatoes and fresh fish. For example, Sicily has been occupied by many different cultures and has influenced their cooking styles significantly. Almonds, couscous, and tomatoes are only a few items brought to the island by their occupiers.

These are some of the different cooking traditions of each of the regions in Italy. These traditions are made based on what ingredients are readily available within their area. Therefore, Italian cuisine does not only mean pasta and pizza because it can offer a wider variety of dishes from different traditions.

Simplicity: Like what was mentioned earlier, Italian cuisines are more attentive to how fresh their ingredients are and not the recipe's complexity. Typical Italian food only requires a few ingredients to create and this is what makes Italians amazing.

The history of Italian cuisine is rooted from generation to generation for each Italian family. Italian people care so much about their family's cooking history that recipes are being passed from one generation to the other by word of mouth. However, as the old get older and the young are not interested until later some have taken to documenting the recipes which is a plus to history and readily available to the world via the internet. It is then the responsibility of the new generation to preserve the traditional recipes and pass them on to the young ones. However, in the general view of the entire Italian food culture, everything started from the ancestors of Italy.

The Romans, which are the greatest ancestors of Italy, adored food so much. Back in the day, Romans loved to feast on food, organizing banquet after banquet just to taste the wonders of the Italian dishes. This is also the best time to serve and introduce new dishes to the table for everyone to try and judge. Rifugio's Country Italian Cuisine has taken this theme and creates feasts based loosely on seasonal events of Italy like "The Feast of the Seven Fishes" or "The Feast of Saint Francis in honor of their ancestors. The Roman empire accepted the flavors of all the ingredients from the places they have conquered. They enjoyed how the spices from the Middle East have enhanced their classic Italian favorites. Romans also started to introduce cereals that they acquired from North Africa and served them on their Italian tables.

If today Italian dishes are only made with fewer ingredients, at the time of the Roman Empire, all their recipes are nothing less than elaborate. From the sophisticated food preparation techniques to intricate choice of ingredients. This is the reality of the Italian food culture back in the days, especially if you are cooking for the rich and famous families in ancient Rome. You must ensure that what you put on their table is the best and nothing less. However, ordinary people still stick to food that suits their living status which is usually a three-ingredient recipe.

Wine, olive oil, and cereals are the most common ingredients Romans used in their simple everyday meal which the current Italian people still use up to this date. When the Barbarians came into the picture, the Roman Empire along with its traditions had come to an end. Traditions from both cultures clash with each other which resulted in one culture influencing the other and vice versa especially when it came to food.

Romans are known to possess sophistication while Barbarians are referred to as harsh-speaking and rugged-looking people. These newcomers introduced beer and butter to the Romans, while the Romans taught the Barbarians about wines and the use of olive oil. In Sicily on the other hand, during the middle ages, the region was colonized by Arabs which influenced their culture and introduced the use of spices and dried fruits to the region. This Arabic influence can still be found in the modern-day dishes from Sicily. Contrary to what everyone assumed, dried pasta does not originate in Italy. It was just brought to Italy by Arabs as they found it easier to transport and preserve, which is suitable for their long journeys at sea.

VEGETABLES FOR ALL SEASONS

Talking of fresh vegetables, there is a very definite pattern as to what you can eat throughout the year.

It's a seasonal thing, with certain vegetables being produced in prolific quantities for a specific spell and then making way for a different selection. So, with Summer coming up, for example, particular favourites include aubergines, beans, beetroot, cucumbers, courgettes, peas, radishes and tomatoes.

When Winter comes again, the colder months bring along the likes of artichokes, broccoli, brussel sprouts, cabbages, cauliflowers, fennel, spinach and turnips.

However, there are still a select few vegetables to be grown throughout all of the year – and these include chicory, lettuce and carrots.

Essential ingredients create the foundation of Italian cuisine.

1. Extra virgin olive oil. While olive oil is often used in cooking, higher quality extra virgin olive oil is used as a garnish to add a peppery flavor. It is also used as a dip for Italian bread like focaccia or drizzled over salad.

2. Balsamic vinegar. True balsamic vinegar is produced in the Italian region of Modena or Emilia-Romagna. This dark, well-aged vinegar is used in marinades and dressings.

3. Garlic. Garlic is one of the most popular ingredients throughout the country, especially sautéed in olive oil to create a flavorful cooking base.

4. Pasta. Pasta is a mix of flour, eggs, olive oil, water, and salt. There are many varieties based on the shape and the region they're from. Popular types include spaghetti (long, thin strands of pasta); penne (tube shapes from Liguria); tagliatelle (thin pasta ribbons from Bologna); fettuccine (long, flat pasta from Rome); and pappardelle (flat, wide pasta ribbons from Tuscany).

5. Pasta sauce. Think marinara (tomatoes, garlic, onion, olive oil, and basil; this is Italy's most famous sauce); Pomodoro (Italian for "tomato," this sauce uses the same ingredients as marinara but is a thicker, smoother sauce); bolognese (meat like pancetta, beef, and lamb are simmered in a tomato and wine sauce); and pesto (basil, garlic, olive oil, pine nuts, and grated parmesan cheese are blended together into a green sauce served over pasta, fish, or spread on bread).

6. Fresh tomatoes. Brought to Italy in the sixteenth century, Italians first thought tomatoes were poisonous. Now they are the heart of Italian cuisine.

7. Oregano. Dried oregano leaves add an earthy flavor to marinara sauce, pizza, salad dressing, or grilled meats.

8. Capers. "Capperi" are pickled flower buds from the Flinders rose bush. These small, salty green orbs are a popular ingredient in Mediterranean

dishes like chicken piccata and puttanesca sauce.

9. Porcini mushrooms. In Italy, porcini mushrooms are found under pine and oak trees, especially in Tuscany. Porcinis, either fresh or dried, are added to sauces cooked in risotto, or simmered in a wine sauce to add texture to a dish.

10. Basil. Basil is a fragrant green herb with a smokey, minty taste, and the most popular herb in Italian cooking. Basil is often used in tomato sauce, in Caprese salad, and is the main ingredient in pesto sauce.

11. Italian cheese. Ancient Romans created varieties of cheese by aging and smoking them. Hard cheeses have a grainy texture and are shaved over salads or grated over pasta. Popular varieties include Parmigiano-Reggiano from Parma in the Emilia-Romagna region and Grana Padano from northern Italy. Pecorino are cheeses made from sheep's milk. A soft cheese like mozzarella is used to melt over meals, like lasagna and pizza.

- Mozzarella: It can be used on all kinds of pastries.
- Parmaggiano: It is also can be used on all kinds of pastries as well.
- Ricotta: Fresh must be consumed. When it is choped and mixed with spinach, gnocchi is made. It is also used in the desserts.
- Mascarpone: Used in all desserts.
- Bel paese: Blue mould cheese.
- Provoloni, pecorino: These cheeses becoming spicy when they are getting dry up.

12. Red wine, white wine. To many, Italy is practically synonymous with wine. Wine has certainly been part of Italian culture at least since the peninsula was colonized by the Ancient Greeks—and thousands of years even before that if recent research is to be believed. Italians drink wine and also use it to simmer meat dishes and add another layer of flavor to a red sauce. Learn more about the different types of wine grapes grown all over the world here.

13. Mint: Widely used. It is used with meat, chicken, salad, sauce and desserts.

14. Marjoram: It is used in soup, dessert, stew and fish. Wild marjoram is also used in the Napolitana pizza. Sweet marjoram can be used instead of oregano, and in Italy goes into soup, stews, and fish dishes. Celery: It is mainly used in vegetable soups. It is rarely served raw, possibly because it appears to be mostly of a rather stringy and thin growth. Daphne: It is used

in soups.

15.Sage: It is widely used in Italian cuisine, especially with veal and calf's liver.

Risotto Alla Milanese: Brought to Sicily by the Moors in the thirteenth century, rice is mostly grown in the fertile lands of northern Italy's Po Valley. Carnaroli or Arborio rice is sautéed with onions in butter, then simmered in saffron-flavored broth and white wine, and topped with parmesan cheese.

Polenta: Polenta is stone-ground corn that is whisked into boiling water or broth, usually in a copper pot, until thick. A classic polenta has butter, black pepper, and parmesan mixed in.

Ravioli: Ravioli is a type of pasta ripiena—stuffed pasta. They are square or round cuts of pasta wrapped around a savory filling, like ricotta cheese with herbs, and served with sauce.

Swordfish: Sicily is known for its seafood, including Sicilian swordfish. This filet is simply cooked in olive oil with capers, sundried tomatoes, and wine.

Parmigiana: This eggplant parmigiana dish consists of breaded eggplant slices fried in olive oil, layered with tomato sauce and mozzarella, and baked.

Arancini: These Sicilian rice balls are made by rolling cooked risotto mixed with butter and parmesan. The balls are dipped in flour, egg, and breadcrumbs, and fried in olive oil until they are golden. They resemble little oranges or "arancini" in Italian.

Ribollita: This Tuscan stew was created when servants would clear the plates of their masters and cook the leftovers in boiling water. Ribollita, which means re-boiled, is made with cannellini beans and hearty vegetables and thickened with stale bread.

Spaghetti Alla Carbonara: This dish from Rome is simply cooked spaghetti tossed into a hot pan with guanciale (pork cheek) or pancetta. A mix of egg, parmesan, and black pepper is poured into the hot pasta.

Lasagna: There are so many different pasta dishes in the Italian cookbook but the best amongst all of them is lasagna. Many years ago, lasagna was known to be a poor man's food but it was transformed to become the most favorite dish on the rich people's table. At Rifugio's Country Italian Cuisine, Washington, we offer our customers the classic lasagna that is bathed with bolognese sauce and topped with parmesan and mozzarella cheese that creates a perfect harmony. This combination of flavors that are crafted using fresh ingredients will burst into your taste buds.

Pizza: Just like with pasta, pizza offers a vast array of options to consumers. However, the most popular choice for many that you must also try is the Pizza Napoletana. This type of pizza originated from Naples and is the perfect example of a classic yet simple Italian recipe. You can see that the Pizza Napoletana only has a few ingredients. Typically, you can only see tomatoes, cheese, and basil on top of the pizza aside from its dough and sauce which are also made from freshly picked tomatoes.

Gelato: When it comes to dessert, Italian food also has something to brag to the world which is gelato. Gelato is not your typical ice cream. Although the Italian people did not invent ice cream, they pride themselves on perfecting the process of ice cream making. The birth of Italian gelato happened during the renaissance period where it was introduced by an alchemist to the Medici family. Today, it is one of the foods that you cannot afford not to taste especially if you visit Italy.

Tiramisu: Another dessert that you must try aside from gelato is the tiramisu. Even though the name sounds a little bit Japanese, it is truly an Italian dessert. Another dish that Rifugio's Country Italian Cuisine can offer your palate is our tiramisu that is enhanced with reduced balsamic vinegar drizzled over top. Balsamic vinegar is not your usual sour vinegar. It has a balance of sweet and sour that will provide an extra kick to the already delicious double chocolate tiramisu. If you visit our restaurant, you must not forget to try this dessert and see how the balsamic vinegar works its magic with the tiramisu.

Osso Buco: If you love meat so much then the Ossobuco would be the best recommendation for you. This hearty dish is the pride of Milan, Italy that was first created during the later part of the 19th century. The traditional recipe of osso buco is made of veal shank. The meat is slowly cooked in meat broth, white wine with vegetables. It is then seasoned with parsley, garlic, and fresh lemon zest. Just by enjoying this dish, all of its flavors will let you experience the rich culture of Milan.

Caprese salad: This popular summer salad is simply tomato slices topped with mozzarella cheese and basil leaves, with a drizzle of olive oil and balsamic vinegar.

Gnocchi: These billowy dumplings are mashed up potatoes mixed with whole grain flour. There are many varieties of Italian gnocchi, each made from different starchy ingredients. This variety originates from the

Lombardy region in Northern Italy and is the most common and well-known variety of gnocchi. It is often mixed with butter and sage

Pesce Spada Agghiotta: It is a stew made of the fish and shellfish.

Cape Sante alla Veneziana: It is a typical dish of the Venetian region. It is made of clam. Clams are found a lot in the Adriatic Sea.

Coffee : Coffee is the most preferred hot drink in Italy. The special Italian coffees are widely used in the world. The espresso coffee which is a thick and hard, is identified with Italy. It is made of a special machine. Cappuccino is made from espresso, hot milk and milk foam made from steam

Italian cuisine is a rich cuisine that varies from region to region. The Italian cuisine, which has been influenced by Etruscan, Ancient Greek, Ancient Roman, Byzantine and Arabic cuisines, has developed with the history and, social and political changes for many years. Today it is known and loved all over the world. Food and dishes and the supplies used for cooking are vary by region. Many of the main dishes of the national cuisine were originally local, then spread all over Italy. There had been some changes during this expansion. Pizza and pasta are essential for the Italian cuisine. In addition to pizza and pasta, cheese and wine make up a large portion of the cuisine with many varieties. Coffee, and especially espresso, is one of the important elements of the Italian cuisine (Volpi, 2003). The distinction could be made between rich and poor cuisine in Italian cuisine. The poor cuisine is only aimed at feeding and at this point it is difficult to talk about the cuisine art. Unlike England, Germany and the United States, when wealth and urbanization increased in Italy, the fast food was not in demand and the interest in traditional meals and small-scale food producers had increased. Home-made meals continued to occupy an important place in the Italian cuisine (Helstosky, 2008). The Italian cuisine has now become a heritage that all Italians have carefully guarded and is trying to be protected from globalization. Unlike European neighbours, Italian cuisine is resisting fast food restaurants (Helstosky, 2004).

CHAPTER FOURTEEN

French Food Festival

French cooking is considered by many to be the most prestigious and respectable cuisine in the world. With its formal techniques, emphasis on fresh ingredients and simple flavors, pride in presentation, and rich and colorful history, French cuisine truly has come to rule the world, laying the foundations for many other styles and specialties.

Music: has always played an important role in French culture as well. There are many different styles, from classical to jazz and everything in between. However, all these styles have harmony, which can be heard throughout France's musical history from medieval times through the modern day. French culture is known for its wide variety and diversity in music, literature, artistry, architecture fashion, among other fields.

The Foundations of French Cooking

French cooking is incredibly complex and is built upon many years of history. Still most chefs would agree that technique, ingredients, and the dining experience are important components of this cuisine.

Technique: French cooking techniques require patience, skill, and attention to detail. These take years to master, but should be studied by all aspiring chefs.

Mise en Place: Mise en place means "everything in its place," and it's a key component of kitchen organization. Before cooking a dish, a chef organizes their tools and prepares, cuts, and measures their ingredients. Everything should be close at hand and ready to go when it's time to cook. A chef must be mentally prepared to execute the techniques to create masterpieces!

Saute: Sauteeing is a technique of cooking ingredients in a pan coated with olive oil or butter over medium to high heat. To sauter means "to jump" in French, which is what ingredients do in a hot pan. One classic dish that relies on this technique is lamb chasseur.

Braise : Braising is a combination cooking method used to cook meat or vegetables in a covered pot over low heat until the products are tender. Chefs typically sear the surface of meat or vegetables at high temperatures then lower the heat. Next, the ingredients slowly cook in fat, stock, or wine to produce complex flavors along with soft and tender bites.

Confit : To confit an ingredient requires salting and cooking the product in fat. Traditionally, this technique was used to preserve meat. Duck confit is a classic French dish that uses this method. However, you can also confit many vegetables such as garlic or potatoes!

Flambe : Flambe involves the use of flammable alcohol to make desserts such as cherries jubilee. When the alcohol is set on fire or flambeed, it burns the alcohol away in mere seconds while leaving the aroma of the liquor's main flavor. For many years, restaurants would flambé various dishes tableside to highlight both the technique and enhance the dining experience for their guests!

Food important to French Culture

The French have a saying that goes, "The stomach rules the mind." It means that if you're hungry, you won't be able to think about anything else. And this is just one reason why food is so important in France. France's culinary art is world-famous and renowned for its quality and variety. Food is almost a national obsession in France. Whenever there are many reasons to celebrate, the French will always find an excuse to gather around food and wine.

It's easy to discover the depth of the French passion for food by visiting many local markets or even supermarkets. You'll see such things as an incredible array of bread, cheeses, oysters, fresh produce with a wide choice of fruits and vegetables, wines, and much more.

Another example of how important food is in France can be seen when you consider their traditional meal times: breakfast at 7:00 AM, lunch at noon, afternoon snack (le goûter) at 3:30 PM (for kids only), dinner around 8:00 PM.

Food is one of the things that France is known for. Some of the most famous and delicious French food includes:

- Baguette - long, thin loaf of bread.
- Boeuf bourguignon - a beef stew cooked in red wine, traditionally Burgundy, and served with potatoes or noodles.

- Cassoulet - a rich stew from Toulouse made from white beans and meat, usually pork sausages and goose.
- Crêpe - a thin pancake made of buckwheat flour and filled with sweet or savory mixtures.
- Croissant - a light roll made with butter and often filled with chocolate or cheese - is typically eaten at breakfast.
- Éclair - a long, thin pastry filled with custard or cream and topped with chocolate icing.
- Foie gras - goose or duck liver pate.
- Fromage frais/fromage Blanc - fresh cheese made from milk (not to be confused with fromage frais/fromage Blanc dessert).
- Jambon-beurre or jambon and pain beurre - ham sandwich on baguette contains literally "ham-butter".
- Pain au chocolat - croissant shaped bread

Ingredients: Another marker of French cuisine that differentiates it from others is the use of high quality ingredients. French dishes often use simple ingredients transformed by artful techniques. Fresh, naturally produced ingredients can always be found in French cuisine. Wine, cheese, olive oil, and seasonal vegetables are just a few staples. Herbs and spices are also important to French cuisine and can contribute a depth of flavor to otherwise subtle dishes. A few commonly used in French dishes include herbs de Provence, tarragon, and nutmeg.

Cured meat (charcuterie): French people standardized cured meat in the 15th century, which largely contributed to putting it on the global map. The most popular types of cured meat are jambon (dried ham) and saucisse (cured sausage). Most regions in France also have their own takes and specialties.

Pork (porc): Pork cuts are slightly different in France. The bacon we know, for instance, is not so common in France. Instead, people tend to have their bacon cut thicker to make lardon. Other common cuts are poitrine (pork belly), échine (the area near the blade bone and spare ribs), épaule (shoulder), and plat de côtes (where the hand and the belly meet). Pork cuts are used in some popular dishes such as chou farci (cabbage leaves stuffed with pork), petit salé aux lentilles (pork stew with lentils), and porc aux pruneaux (roast pork with prunes).

Lamb (agneau): Some cuts that are specific to lamb include gigot d'agneau (leg of lamb), collet (scrag), poitrine (breast), côtelette (cutlet), and selle d'agneau (saddle). Some famous recipes made with lamb are navarin (stew with veggies and lamb), gigot d'agneau pleureur (lamb roast), and clapassade (simmered lamb with olives, honey, and star anise).

Beef (bœuf): Common cuts of beer include bifteck (steak), bavette (undercut), steak haché (ground beef), romsteak (rump steak), and entrecôte (ribeye). Besides the world-famous châteaubriand, steak tartare, and steak frites, there is a wealth of French beef recipes.

Poultry (volaille): The French diet encompasses every type of poultry you can imagine. Usually, French people buy their poultry, including lapin (rabbit), from specialty shops. Other types of poultry include poulet (chicken), coq (cockerel), dinde (turkey), and volaille (fowl). Some popular French poultry recipes include coq au vin (rooster stew with red wine), confit de canard (slow-roasted duck), magret de canard (seared duck breast), among others.

Offal (abats) and game (gibier): If you're feeling adventurous, then you'll be glad to know that French cuisine features a variety of offal and game meat dishes. In fact, these are staples in kitchens throughout Lyon, which is widely considered to be the gastronomic capital of France with its famous neighborhood bouchons.

Fish and seafood in France: With coastlines meeting the Mediterranean Sea and the Atlantic Ocean, it's no surprise that French cuisine incorporates a lot of fish and seafood. People throughout the country enjoying eating everything from moule (mussel) and coquilles Saint-Jacques (scallops) to anguilles (eels) and seiche (cuttlefish).

Some other common types of fish and seafood in France include the following:

- Homard (lobster) – used in creamy and spicy bisque soup and the extravagant lobster Thermidor
- Rascasse (red scorpionfish) – used in the luxurious bouillabaisse, which can set you back a hefty €200 when eaten as a meal for two
- Carpe (carp) – used together with other freshwater fish in the classic matelote stew
- Lotte (monkfish) – used in bourride, aka bouillabaisse's cousin, which is made with white fish

Vegetables in France: Like its Dutch almost-neighbor, France enjoys its potatoes, and these are a staple of its cuisine. In fact, according to Statista,

57% of the French population named pomme de terre (potato) as their favorite vegetable in 2018. Other popular options include tomate (tomato), carotte (carrot), endive (chicory), courgette (zucchini), and oignon (onion). In fact, two of the most famous French dishes are vegetable-based: the colorful ratatouille and soupe à l'oignon, which has warmed souls since Roman times.

Fruits in France: Since Roman times, fraise (strawberry) has been considered a symbol of Venus, the Goddess of Love, and associated with love and romance. It should come as no surprise, therefore, that it is the most popular fruit in France. Pomme (apple), pêche (peach), banane (banana), melon (melon), orange (orange), clémentine (clementine), cerise (cherry), and framboise (raspberry), follow it, respectively. Raisin (grape), on the other hand, are not as popular and are generally preferred in their liquid, head-spinning form.

Herbs and spices in France: French cooking is all about elegance and simplicity, and using quality ingredients that are in season is key. Although French cuisine doesn't rely too much on spices, they are still used to add a layer of flavor and to highlight the main ingredient in the dishes. In addition to noix de muscade (nutmeg) and safran (saffron), popular spices include the following:

- Fines herbes – translated as delicate herbs, fines herbes refer to ciboulette (chives), persil (parsley), estragon (tarragon), and cerfeuil (chervil). These require a shorter cooking time and are added to delicate ingredients such as chicken, fish, and eggs.
- Persillade – made from chopped parsley, garlic, oil, and vinegar, you can use this seasoning mix to bring flavor to anything from fish to roasted potatoes... and snails.
- Herbes de Provence – possibly the most well-known of spice mixes, Herbes de Provence combines marjolaine (marjoram), romarin (rosemary), thym (thyme), origan (oregano), and sometimes even lavande (lavender) to enrich your stews – and Ratatouille.
- Bouquet garni – more of a cooking method, bouquet garni ("garnished bouquet") is a bundle of herbs tied together with string to flavor soups, stocks, stews, and casseroles. Don't forget to take it out before wolfing down your delectable creation, though!

Famous Cheese

Reblochon: Reblochon is a soft, creamy cheese that originates from the snowy French Alps. This rich cheese is made from unpasteurized cow's milk and has a strong, pungent flavor.

Brie: Brie is a soft cheese that you make from cow's milk. The French people from the province of Brie invented this cheese, hence its name. Brie has a mild, buttery flavor and a smooth, creamy texture. The rind of Brie is edible and has a nutty flavor. It owes its richness to the high levels of butterfat used to make it.

Pont l'Evèque: Pont l'Evèque is a soft, washed-rind cheese from France's Normandy region. It is made from unpasteurized cow's milk and has a strong, pungent flavor.

Munster: Munster is a stinky and soft cheese with a delicate flavor. The French produce it in the Alsace region. It is made from unpasteurized cow's milk and has a strong, pungent taste.

Roquefort: Roquefort is a blue cheese born in the Roquefort-Sur-Soulzon region of France. It is made from unpasteurized sheep's milk and has a strong, salty flavor.

Mont d'Or: Mont d'Or is a seasonal cheese best enjoyed in winter. This delicate and rich cheese comes from the Franche-Comté region of France. It is made from unpasteurized cow's milk and has a mild, nutty flavor. This cheese comes from the Monts d'Or mountain in the Franche-Comté region.

Camembert: Camembert is a moist, soft cow's milk cheese. The French first produced it in the 18th century in the Normandy region of France, specifically in the town of Camembert.

Epoisses: Epoisses is a soft, stinky cheese first produced in the Burgundy region of France.

Bleu d'Auvergne: Blue cheese is my favorite type of cheese, and Bleu d'Auvergne.

Comté: Comté is a hard, Alpine-style cheese that emerged from the Franche-Comté region of France.

Cantal: Cantal is a hard, raw cow's milk cheese that was first produced in the Auvergne region of France. It has the distinction of being one of the oldest cheeses in France.

Fourme d'Ambert: Fourme d'Ambert is a semi-hard, blue cheese from France's Auvergne region.

Brocciu: Brocciu is a Corsican cheese made from the milk of sheep and whey. It has a creamy, slightly salty flavor.

Saint Nectaire: Saint Nectaire is a cow's milk cheese from the Auvergne region of France. It has a soft, creamy texture and a delightful creamy color.

Pélardon: Pélardon is a traditional goat's milk cheese from the Languedoc-Roussillon region of France.

Dining Experience: Another foundation of French cuisine is the dining experience, which requires careful presentation, elegance, and community when eating. A version of this could be seen all the way back in the Middle Ages at the banquets held by the aristocracy, but French cooking underwent many changes to end up where it is today. With the rise of haute cuisine, meals became smaller and presentations became more detailed and elegant. Nouvelle cuisine placed even greater emphasis on precision in presentation. Today, many chefs in fine dining restaurants are as talented at presenting their food as they are at preparing it!

Sauces and condiments in France

- French chef Marie-Antoine Carême is known as the founder of haute cuisine and published L'art de la cuisine française au dix-neuvième siècle in the 19th century. In his book, he identifies what he calls sauces mères (mother sauces), which are a group of sauces that a lot of other petites sauces ("daughter" sauces) around the world are based on. Here are some of them:
- Béchamel – this rich and creamy versatile sauce that we all know and love is generally made by mixing flour and butter (roux) with cream. It is traditionally used in pasta, lasagna, and gratin dishes.
- Velouté – like béchamel, the base of this sauce is roux, which is then mixed with animal stock. You can enrich velouté by adding different ingredients to create variations, such as allemande (with heavy cream and lemon juice) and cardinal (with lobster butter and cayenne pepper).
- Espagnole – this is a flavor-heavy mother sauce, which is made by mixing dark brown roux with beef or veal stock, tomato sauce, and mirepoix (chopped carrots, celery, and onions). You can use this sauce to give your soups, stews, and meat dishes more body.
- Sauce tomate – arguably the most commonly used mother sauce, this is generally made by mixing onions, garlic, and tomatoes. If you feel fancy, though, you can also experiment with salted pork breast, mirepoix, and white stock. This versatile sauce is used in various dishes ranging from pizza to shakshuka.

- Hollandaise – originally mentioned as a daughter sauce in Carême's book, Hollandaise uses emulsification to bind butter and lemon juice together with egg yolks. It requires more effort to make, but the reward is a fancier take on mayonnaise that can be used in dishes such as eggs Benedict.

Famous dishes

Salmon En Papillote : This dish is called, in English, "Salmon in Parchment." It is perhaps one of the most unique ways to cook a fish. Essentially, you wrap the salmon and vegetables inside a piece of parchment, and you let them all cook together. What happens is that each individual flavor—juices and all—blend together to form a delicious meal. This is a very famous French food that you should definitely consider trying if you travel to France. Additionally, even if you don't plan to travel to France anytime soon, this dish would make an excellent option for when you have friends and family over for dinner.

Confit de Canard: Confit de canard is a tasty and flavorful duck dish. The duck is cooked in its own fat for a long period together with spices like thyme and garlic, which gives the dish a unique flavor. Confit de canard is a French dish that is typically served as a main course, and it is often eaten with mashed potatoes or chips.

Foie Gras: If you are looking for a unique and flavorful French dish, then Foie gras probably makes the mark. Foie gras is a French dish with goose or duck liver. It is typically served on bread. The production method is a controversial topic but it remains a popular dish for holiday seasons.

Cassoulet: Cassoulet is a French stew that is made with white beans, meat (usually pork, duck, sausage), and vegetables. It is named after the cassole, a clay pot in which it is cooked. Cassoulet has been around for centuries and is a traditional French food. It can be eaten as a main course or as an accompaniment to another dish. It is a heartwarming dish that is perfect for cold winter days and will leave you feeling satisfied.

Pâté de Campagne: Pâté de Campagne is a French dish made with pork and spices grounded together. It is a nice appetizer and often goes with a French baguette or crackers. The dish dates back to the Middle Ages and is popular in the European countryside.

Poulet à la Crème: Poulet à la crème is a French dish featuring a combination of chicken and cream. The chicken is usually cooked in a white wine sauce, and the dish is seasoned with herbs and spices. Poulet à la crème is a French dish that is typically served as a main course, and it is often eaten with Chips or bread.

Steak frites: Voila – this simple, yet impressive recipe is inspired by French bistro cuisine.

Chicken confit: In this classic confit, the chicken is salted and seasoned with herbs, then slowly cooked in olive oil to make it rich and tender.

Soupe à L'oignon (French onion soup): See out the winter with this fragrant French onion soup. Don't forget the cheesy croutons.

Moules Marinières: Moules Marinières is a French dish that is made with mussels and white wine. The mussels are usually cooked in a garlic butter sauce, and the dish is seasoned with herbs and spices. Moules Marinières is a French dish that great for seafood lovers. It can be a main course with a carbs pairing or is also good for sharing as an appetizer.

Bouillabaisse: Bouillabaisse is a French seafood dish that is made with a variety of different types of seafood. Some consider it to be the national dish of France, and it is definitely one of the most popular French dishes.

Ratatouille: Ratatouille is a French dish that is made with vegetables, and it is usually served as a side dish. The vegetables in ratatouille are cooked in olive oil, and the dish is seasoned with herbs and spices. Ratatouille is one of the most famous food in France, much credit to the animation movie. You can pair it with French bread to make a substantial meal. Ratatouille is perfect for those who love vegetables, and the dish is full of flavor and nutrients. Ratatouille is a great option for summer, as it is light and refreshing.

Quiche Lorraine: Quiche Lorraine is a French dish that is made with custard and cheese filling, and usually also consists of meat and vegetables. It has been around since the middles ages, and it is one of the most famous foods in France that people enjoy. Quiche Lorraine is said to have originated in the Lorraine region of France, and it is a very popular dish in that region.

Escargots: Escargots are a French delicacy featuring snails cooked in butter, parsley, and garlic. They can be eaten as a main course or appetizer. Escargots are said to have originated in France, and they are a popular French food that is enjoyed by many.

Flamiche: Flamiche is a French tart that is made with leeks and cream. There can also be other vegetable stuffings. You can have this as a filling meal or a nice snack. Flamiche has its origins in the Picardy region and sometimes referred to as Flamique by the locals.

Salmon en papillote: This clever technique of wrapping fish in paper before cooking ensures that all the moisture and flavours are locked in.

Quiche – the savory cousin of pie, quiche is essentially a pastry filled with eggs and cream mixed with meat, cheese, vegetables, or seafood. You can make your own version by adding any hearty ingredients your heart desires. The most famous recipe is Quiche Lorraine, which is made from bacon.

Gratin Dauphinois – hailing from southeastern France, this baked potato dish is the crown jewel of the winter dinner table. You can make your own version by combining layers of sliced potatoes with milk and cream, topped with breadcrumbs or grated cheese.

Croque monsieur – this fancy French take on the grilled cheese sandwich consists of two slices of bread dipped in egg batter, with ham in between, and topped with melted Gruyère cheese. You can take your croque monsieur to god-tier by serving it with béchamel sauce!

Boeuf bourguignon: Boeuf bourguignon is a great example of budget cuts of meat being turned into stylish haute cuisine. For authenticity, be sure to use a Burgundian pinot noir for this recipe.

Lamb shank navarin: Navarin is a French lamb ragout (or stew). The lamb is cooked low and slow until it melts in the mouth.

Hazelnut dacquoise: With layers of nutty meringue and rich whipped filling, the classic French cake dacquoise – pronounced dah-kwahz- is so impressive.

Croque Madame: Croque Madame is a popular French dish that is made up of ham and cheese sandwiched between two slices of bread and then grilled. The dish usually comes with a fried egg on top. Croque Madame is a popular French dish that is also a regular in restaurants.

Tarte tatin: Was this creation the result of a mistake in the kitchen or did the Tatin sisters plan on baking their apple tart upside down? We'll never know the real story but with a buttery base, rich fillings, caramelised fruits and lashings of syrup, this sweet tart is in a class of its own.

Souffle: These light-as-air desserts are nothing short of irresistible.

Paris-brest: Cousin to the croquembouche, this custard-frilled choux pastry ring is like a giant chocolate eclair.

Croque Madame and Croque Monsieur: Basically a grilled ham and cheese sandwich. A croque madame is simply a croque monsieur with a poached or fried egg on top and béchamel sauce. With a Croque Monsieur, the bread is dipped into a beaten egg (like a savoury French Toast) before cooking.

Coq au Vin: The classic French dish that many experienced in Canada for the first time on their trip to Quebec. Originally Coq au vin was made from a coq, or old rooster, and red wine. The tough meat of the rooster was tenderized by the slow, stew-like cooking technique. The rich flavour of the wine permeates the meat, which is garnished with mushrooms and onions.

Galettes and Crepes: Galettes are savory crepes made with buckwheat flour and served with a saucisse (French sausage) or wrapped around ham and eggs or other savoury French favourites. Crepes are the sweet versions and served with lemon and sugar, Nutella and banana or salted caramel for a classic French flavour

Crème brûlée – a scene-stealer in the French film Amélie, this custard-based dessert combines egg yolk, sugar, vanilla, and heavy cream. The key to a perfect crème brûlée, however, is its caramelized sugar crust which makes a satisfying crunch sound when broken.

Macaron – hailing from the Renaissance era, the fashionable macaron is a meringue-based cookie sandwich that comes in a myriad of flavors ranging from raspberry and lemon to Mexican spice and lavender.

Canelé – originating in the region of Bordeaux, the canelé currently reigns supreme in every pâtisserie in France. The caramel-crusted rich pastry is made using rum and vanilla but has a pleasantly surprising creamy custard center.

Pain au chocolat: French pain au chocolat is a type of pastry that is made with chocolate and dough. It is usually eaten as a breakfast food, and it is one of the most popular French pastries. The dough is made with flour, salt, sugar, eggs, and butter. The chocolate can be in the form of a filling or it can be melted and used as a topping. French pain au chocolat is a delicious pastry that you should definitely try if you are in France.

Lobster Bisque: French chefs are masters at creating fantastic soups that have become icons on dinner tables worldwide. A well-known favorite is the traditional lobster bisque. This seafood recipe is the epitome of a creamy-style soup, and it can easily become the centerpiece of a light meal. The fresh lobster meat is surrounded by a rich broth tinged with Cognac, giving the bisque a complex and unique taste.

Cognac Shrimp With Beurre Blanc: We cannot discuss French cuisine without mentioning the combination of shallots, wine, cream, butter, and cognac. These ingredients come together in this delightful main dish that's easy to cook up. The name of this Cognac shrimp recipe makes it sound fancier and perhaps more difficult to make than it is in reality—a beurre blanc is simply a butter and wine sauce. You'll be delighted when you see how short and common the ingredient list is. It's possible you have everything you need already in your kitchen.

French Crepes: If you are looking for a French dish that is a little bit lighter, then you may want to try the French dish of crepes. Crepes are thin pancakes that are usually made with wheat flour, and they can be filled with different things. Some of the most popular fillings for crepes are chocolate, fruit, and cheese. Crepes are a very popular breakfast food in France, and they are often served with a cup of tea or coffee

Palmiers: the delightfully sweet, flaky cookies also known as elephant ears . The palmiers are not unlike the flaky texture of a croissant but are in fact made with puff pastry.

CHAPTER FIFTEEN

Japanese Food Festival

Japanese food is one of the most popular cuisines in the world and for good reason. Based on "rules of five," traditional Japanese cooking, or washoku, emphasizes variety and balance. This is achieved through the use of five colors (black, white, red, yellow, and green), five cooking techniques (raw food, grilling, steaming, boiling, and frying), and five flavors (sweet, spicy, salty, sour, and bitter). These principles can be found even in a single meal of one soup and three sides paired with rice.

Traditionally, chefs in training are not allowed to handle the fish or meat for years. The primary chef creates all the food while the apprentice does other tasks like clean, preparation, and serving tables. A truly traditional restaurant won't have a serving staff as this is the responsibility of the apprentice.

In Japan, the dishes are nearly as important as the food they contain. The cooks are careful to choose the right colors and patterns for the meal they're preparing. Plates and bowls are often seasonal, hand-painted, and have a significant history. The servers and chef often expect people to ask about the dishes before eating.

INGREDIENTS

1. SOY SAUCE: Soy sauce is one of the most basic flavourings in Japanese cuisine. When cooking Japanese food you use soy sauce instead of salt to add savory flavour. Soy sauce is made from brewed fermented soy beans, and you can use it as a dipping sauce too. Generally it's mixed with rice wine vinegar, mirin and sometimes chilli, ginger or spring onions to create a base for many dishes.

2. RICE VINEGAR: Rice wine vinegar is of course, used for seasoning rice. To make perfectly seasoned sushi rice, you need to heat a pan of rice wine vinegar, 1 Tbsp of Sugar and 1 Tsbp of salt gently, until the sugar dissolves. You then pour this over the rice and stir well. Rice wine vinegar

can also be used with soy sauce to make a dipping sauce which is great with oily fried foods like gyoza.

3. MIRIN: Mirin is a sweet rice wine which is used to add a slight sweetness to dishes. You'll often find it added to soup stocks, or to dumpling filling mixes.

4. SUSHI RICE: Sushi rice is a good all-round rice to have in the cupboard when cooking Japanese food. It's got a short grain, and gets sticky and glutinous when cooked. This is great if you're eating rice with chopsticks as it will clump together. Sushi rice is great for sushi but also goes well with Japanese curries and can be used to make onigiri.

5. MISO PASTE: Miso paste is also a product of fermented soy beans, and it is often mixed with sea salt and rice to make a paste. This is the basis of miso soup, but it's also a great base for broths or for adding a great flavour to meats.

6. WAKAME: Wakame is a seaweed often used in Japanese cuisine. You'll often find it used in miso soup. It comes in dried form usually, and is softened by adding it to hot water. It's a great addition to any Japanese soup or broth as it has a subtle, sweet flavour and lots of vitamin power!

7. BONITO FLAKES: The bonito fish is a tiny variety of tuna, which is often dried then shaved into thin flakes which are used as the basis for many Japanese broths. The flavour is not overpowering or like tuna, and when heated in water to make dashi stock, bonito provides umami. It's a good idea to keep a stock of ready made dashi in your fridge!

8. KOMBU: Kombu is another element in Japanese dashi stock. It is a type of dried seaweed kelp, and the Japanese age it for great flavours. You will find in Japan Kombu maturing is a serious business, and the best restaurants always have a favourite trusted supplier.

9. SHICHIMI TOGARISHI: Shichimi Togarishi is a spice mix that provides a sweet chilli heat. Use it on almost anything to add a little kick!

10. NORI: Nori is another dried, edible seaweed. This is the stuff which is often used to wrap maki sushi rolls, but you'll also find it cut up as a topping on ramen and soups.

11. NOODLES: You should also keep a variety of dried and vacuum packed noodles in your cupboard; these keep in date for ages so are very practical! Udon noodles and soba noodles are very popular for their taste and texture. Create a soup from chillies, ginger, garlic, dashi stock, soy sauce and rice wine vinegar then add noodles and veggies for a quick Japanese dinner!

12. WASABI: Wasabi is a paste made from a Japanese variety of horseradish. Real wasabi is very expensive as the root is very difficult to farm correctly, so most cheaper wasabi pastes are actually horseradish! The top sushi restaurants will have real wasabi freshly grated from the root into a paste. It's a firey accompaniment to sushi, but also great with meats

13. Dashi powder: Dashi is the cooking and soup stock that is the heart of the Japanese cooking. It's typically made with kombu (sea kelp) and katsuobushi (dried bonito flakes). Dashi or dashi powder, if you ever see it in the recipe, is never optional. While it is possible to make dashi from scratch, one convenient ingredient you should have on hand is the dashi powder. Dashi power can be used to make the dashi soup stock and sometimes it will be added directly with other ingredients just like bouillon powders.

14. Rice vinegar: Rice vinegar is made from fermented rice. The flavor tends to be milder and on the little sweeter side compared to the regular vinegar. The delicate flavor of this vinegar goes perfectly with the Japanese cooking. When you are purchasing rice vinegar, be sure to NOT to pick up the seasoned or flavored variations unless the recipe specifically calls for it. Seasoned rice vinegar contains additional sugar and salt. And for basic cooking purposes, it's best to use the unseasoned rice vinegar (it may also say "sugar free/sodium free" or "natural" on the label) and adjust the flavor as needed.

15. Sesame oil: There are so many types of sesame oil out in the market. But to make the Japanese dishes, it is recommended, of course, to use the Japanese brands. Japanese sesame oil tends to be lighter in color, taste and texture compared to some of the other brands.

The Basics

Rice: Sticky, short-grained rice is the staple food in Japan. Uncooked rice is called kome. The cultivation of rice in paddy fields traditionally required great cooperation between villagers and this is said to have been central to the evolution of Japanese culture. Their are several thousand varieties grown in Japan, with Koshihikari and Akita Komachi being among the most popular. Rice is also used to make mochi (rice cakes), senbei (rice crackers) and sake (rice wine). Rice can also be cooked with red beans (sekihan), seafood and vegetables (Takikomi gohan) or as a kind of watery porridge seasoned with salt (kayu) which is very popular as a cold remedy. Onigiri are rice balls with seafood or vegetables in the middle, usually wrapped in a piece of dried seaweed (nori). They are traditionally part of a packed lunch or picnic. Individually wrapped onigiri, usually a trianular shape, make a good snack and are available at convenience stores.

Noodles - Udon and soba: Udon noodles are made from wheat flour. They are boiled and served in a broth, usually hot but occasionally cold in summer, and topped with ingredients such as a raw egg to make tsukimi udon, and deep-fried tofu aburaage to make kitsune udon. Soba is buckwheat noodles, which are thinner and a darker color than udon. Soba is usually served cold (zaru soba) with a dipping sauce, sliced green onions and wasabi. When served in a hot broth, it is known as kake soba. Served with the same toppings as udon, you get tsukimi soba, kitsune soba and tempura soba.

Noodles - Ramen: While udon and soba are also believed to have come from China, only ramen retains its image as Chinese food. Ramen is thin egg noodles which are almost always served in a hot broth flavored with shoyu or miso. This is topped with a variety of ingredients such as slices of roast pork (chashu), bean sprouts (moyashi), sweetcorn and butter. Ramen is popular throughout Japan and different regions are known for their variations on the theme. Examples are Corn-butter Ramen in Sapporo and Tonkotsu Ramen in Kyushu. Instant ramen (the most famous brand is Pot Noodles), to which you just add hot water, has become very popular in recent years.

Seafood & Meat: Japanese people consume a lot more fish than is typical in western countries and this is said to be a major factor in the country's relatively low rate of heart disease. Seafood is eaten in just about any form you can imagine, from raw sushi and sashimi to grilled sweetfish and clams. The spread of ¥100 kaitenzushi (conveyor belt sushi) restaurants has made sushi into a homegrown fast-food that offsets some of the influence of imports like McDonalds.Many people are surprised to learn that meat consumption was illegal in Japan until the ban was lifted during the Meiji Restoration in the 1870s. As the country opened up to western culture, eating habits also began to change. Now meat is increasingly part of the everyday Japanese diet, with yakitori (grilled chicken), yakiniku (Korean barbeque), gyudon (beef bowl) and of course the standard fare of foreign and local hamburger chain restaurants ubiquitous across the country. This has led to an increase in related health problems, though the Japanese still maintain their position as the world's longest-living people.

Soy products: The humble soybean (daizu) is used to make a wide variety of foods and flavourings. Soybeans and rice are used to make miso, a paste used for flavouring soup and marinating fish. Together with soy sauce (shoyu), miso is a foundation of Japanese cuisine. Tofu is soybean curd and a popular source of protein, especially for vegetarians. These days, even tofu donuts and tofu icecream are available. Natto, fermented soybeans, is one of the healthiest but also the most notorious item on the menu. With a pungent smell and sticky, stringy texture, natto is easy to hate straight away. Japanese people themselves tend to either love it or hate it. It is usually served with chopped onions and a raw egg and mixed into a bowl of rice.

Japanese Food

Sushi: Sushi is, without doubt, one of the most famous foods to come from Japan. A dish that was born in ancient times, sushi originated from the process of preserving fish in fermented rice. Today it's made with vinegared rice and fresh fish, presented in a number of ways and shapes.

Tempura: Tempura is a dish of battered and fried fish, seafood, or vegetables. Special care is given to the way the ingredients are cut as well as to the temperature of the batter (ice cold) and oil (very hot) for deep-frying, so that every piece is a bite of crisply fried perfection. In the Kanto region around Tokyo, tempura is eaten with a dipping sauce, while in the Kansai region around Kyoto and Osaka it's dipped in flavored salt.

Yakitori: Yakitori is a dish of bite-sized cuts of chicken grilled on a skewer. It makes use of every part of the chicken — including heart, liver, and even chicken comb — to avoid wastefulness, an important element of Japanese food culture. Unlike other traditional Japanese foods, yakitori has only been eaten since around the mid-17th century, as eating meat was largely taboo in Japan for several centuries.

Tsukemono pickles: Tsukemono are traditional pickles that have been eaten in Japan since prehistoric times. Made with a wide variety of ingredients, including vegetables like daikon radish and eggplant, as well as fruits like ume plum. Tsukemono not only add visual appeal to a meal with their bright colors, they're also an extremely healthy food.

Kaiseki: The ultimate in Japanese fine dining, kaiseki is a tasting course comprised of small, seasonally themed dishes crafted with the utmost precision and attention to detail. Kaiseki was born from the traditional tea ceremony, where small morsels of food were offered alongside the bitter green tea, and over time these offerings evolved into a multi-course haute cuisine meal.

Udon: Udon is a dense and chewy noodle made from wheat flour. It's one of the most popular foods in Japan due to its delicious taste, inexpensive price point, and versatility – udon can be eaten hot or cold and customized with any number of toppings. There are three famous regional varieties of udon noodle: sanuki udon from Kagawa prefecture in Southwest Japan, kishimen from Nagoya in Central Japan, and inaniwa udon from Akita in Northern Japan.

Soba: Soba is another type of noodle dish that has been eaten in Japan for centuries. Made from buckwheat flour, soba has a long thin shape and firm texture and is very healthy. Like udon noodles, soba can be served in a hot broth or chilled with a dipping sauce, making it a delicious and healthy option any time of year.

Sukiyaki: Sukiyaki is a one-pot dish of beef, vegetables, and tofu cooked with a sweet soy sauce broth in a shallow cast iron pot. It became highly popular after the centuries-long ban on eating meat was lifted during the Meiji period, and is the perfect way to enjoy Japan's incredibly rich and tender wagyu beef.

Sashimi: Centuries before Japanese people were eating sushi, they first enjoyed raw fish without the rice. While the name "sashimi" refers to any thinly sliced raw food, including raw beef (gyuu-sashi), chicken (tori-zashi), and even horse (basashi), fish and seafood are the most popular varieties.

Miso soup: Miso soup may seem deceptively simple, but it's an essential Japanese food that's served with any traditional meal. The soup is made from dashi stock – either fish or kelp stock – combined with miso bean paste to bring a savory umami element to any meal. Tofu and sliced green onions, as well as ingredients like fish, clams, and pork, can be added and may vary by the season.

Onigiri: The savior of many a famished salaryman, these rice balls (the Japanese equivalent of a sandwich) can be found on the shelves of every convenience store — far and away the most convenient choice for a meal on the go. This has been the case as far back as 2000 years ago when laborers and fishermen carried pressed rice balls around in their packs. The current form of onigiri can be traced back to the Edo period when the edible seaweed wrapping was introduced. Inside, you'll usually find salty fish fillings, pickled plum, or more modern additions like teriyaki chicken.

Wagashi: These traditional sweets are the jewels of Japanese food culture. The wagashi (Japanese sweets) category is incredibly broad, basically referring to all regional, seasonal, and commonplace traditional Japanese sweets. Starting off in ancient times as very basic creations of mochi rice cakes (a sticky dough made from steamed and crushed rice) that were filled with nuts, these sweets evolved into ornate delicacies made to accompany the traditional matcha green tea ceremonies of the Edo period. Common types of wagashi include taiyaki (a fish-shaped pancake filled with anko or custard), dorayaki (an anko pancake sandwich), daifuku (mochi bites with various fillings), and namagashi (beautifully hand-molded rice flour and anko sweets).

Natto: Legend has it that this divisive dish was invented by accident in the 11th century when the samurai Minamoto no Yoshiie left cooked soybeans in a straw bag on his horse's back which had fermented by the time he got around to eating them. Many people would say he just should've thrown them away. Natto is the Japanese equivalent of marmite — you'll either love it or hate it. Despite its pungent smell, natto is a popular breakfast food. It's also incredibly healthy due to the effect the bacteria has on the boiled soybeans, said to benefit heart health, digestive health, and bone strength.

Oden : This popular winter comfort food started out in the Muromachi period as a stewed tofu dish. Nowadays, other ingredients are added to the bone-warming oden broth, such as fish cakes, potatoes, boiled eggs, daikon radish, and other assorted vegetables. They're usually simmered for several hours to infuse the ingredients with the flavor fully. The rich-yet-mild broth itself typically consists of dried bonito (skipjack tuna) flakes and dried kombu (kelp).Shabu Shabu: This is far and away the most modern dish on the list, invented in 1952 at a restaurant in Osaka. You'd be forgiven for mistaking it for sukiyaki. After all, both are hot pot dishes in which you cook thinly-cut beef strips alongside vegetables. There are a few key differences though. Shabu shabu is cooked in a deeper pot with a milder and more savory broth. It's also common practice to only partially cook the meat in a shabu shabu hot pot, and raw egg isn't used as a dipping sauce.

Ramen: The premise for ramen is deceptively simple: soup stock, flavorings, seasonings, wheat noodles, and toppings (usually fatty pork and vegetables such as bamboo shoots). However, within this simple formula, there's massive room for interpretation. The huge variety can be pretty overwhelming, but we've got a comprehensive ramen guide to reference for your journey into the world of Japanese cusine. You'll find instant ramen packets in supermarkets worldwide, but if you're really serious about trying this dish, head along to any of the ten-thousand-plus local eateries across Japan that prepare it with fresh noodles, rich broths (miso, salt, soy, and tonkotsu being the main types), and generous helpings of toppings.

Tonkatsu: As with many of the things we consider to be quintessentially Japanese, that's only half the story of this breaded pork cutlet dish. Tonkatsu was invented at a Tokyo restaurant called Rengatei in 1899, served with rice and shredded cabbage. It was originally considered a Western-style dish due to the use of pork, which the Japanese rarely ate. On top of that, the Japanese curry sauce added to make the popular katsu curry was introduced to Japan by the British via India.

Kaiseki: A type of cuisine, rather than a food, this style of fine dining has its roots in the courtly culture of imperial Kyoto in the 16th century, when visiting samurai and dignitaries were treated to a series of small dishes to accompany traditional tea ceremonies. Today, anywhere from around 12 to 20 dishes feature in a typical kaiseki meal, with the exact offerings varying according to the season, the chef's expertise, and how strictly they adhere to orthodoxy.

Kappo Ryori : Following the theme of Japanese cuisines, kappo ryori is a style of dining that originated in Osaka, offering a more casual counterpart to Kyoto's kaiseki cuisine. Like kaiseki cuisine, kappo ryori utilizes seasonal and fresh ingredients; but whereas kaiseki dishes are generally prepared in a kitchen and then brought to your private room, kappo ryori is cooked by the chef right in front of their guests.

Shojin Ryori: Ever wondered how Buddhist monks eat? Their diet consists of mainly vegetarian cuisine (think lots of beans and bean-based products), and in Japan, even laypeople can enjoy a sophisticated Buddhist cuisine feast called shojin ryori. With subtle flavors, the meal features fresh mountain vegetables and nutty-tasting goma (sesame) tofu, among other dishes. Rice, soup, pickled vegetables, tofu, and a variety of sides form a well-balanced shojin ryori feast.

Osechi Ryori : Osechi ryori, symbolic Japanese New Year dishes, rolls around like clockwork every year, a feast for the first of January. It comes in a multi-tiered jubako (lacquerware box) and is filled with a variety of foods, each with its own special meaning. For example, the gold-colored kuri-kinton (mashed sweet potatoes with chestnuts) promises wealth, while the hunchbacked boiled shrimp represent old age and longevity. This array of dishes is often enjoyed through the first, second, and third of January, until every last bite is gone–allowing the usual cook of the household to relax for the first few days of the new year.

Zenzai / Oshiruko : Another typical fare during the Japanese New Year, zenzai (also known as oshiruko) is a sweet Japanese red bean soup with mochi. Usually served warm with toasted squares of mochi submerged in the broth, it's a tasty wintertime sweet that's also easy to make at home, this oshiruko recipe is a testament to that!

Wagyu : Wagyu (literally "Japanese beef) is famed worldwide for its meticulous high standards, beautiful marbling of fat, and rich flavor. It can be cooked as a slab of steak, thinly sliced and swish-swished through hot shabu-shabu broth, or boiled in a sukiyaki hotpot and coated in a sauce of raw egg. The Japanese Beef Association strictly regulates all wagyu beef, and grades every cut of beef according to its marbling and yield. There are particular regional brands of wagyu in Japan that are highly coveted, like Matsusaka beef and Kobe beef.

Bento : Creativity, convenience, and color merge in the homemade Japanese bento. In recent years, this classic Japanese packed lunch has gained recognition for its adorable aesthetics, oftentimes featuring rice molded into cute characters and ingredients cut out into cute shapes.

Omurice: A Japanese home cooking staple, omurice is a comfort food that evokes childhood. Made with ketchup fried rice blanketed in an eggy omelet and decorated with a cute ketchup message or design, omurice is a favorite among children and nostalgic adults alike. Check out our omurice recipe to learn how to make it for yourself!

Kiritanpo: A traditional Japanese food that hails from Akita prefecture, kiritanpo is made of pounded rice that is shaped around wooden cylinders and toasted over a hearth. It can be slathered in a sweet miso sauce and eaten right off the skewer; or removed from the cylinder, chopped, and placed into soups.

Mochi: If you know anything about traditional Japanese foods, you're definitely familiar with the chewy, bouncy, stretchy mochi. It's a type of rice cake that takes seemingly infinite forms: from red bean-filled daifuku mochi to toasty soybean powder-dusted kinako mochi, to savory applications like pillowy mochi dumplings in ozoni (Japanese New Year soup).

Gyoza: The perfect side dish at a ramen restaurant, gyoza is the crispy-on-the-outside, juicy-on-the-inside pan-fried dumplings with Chinese origins. In Japanese, gyoza usually contains pork, finely-chopped cabbage, and mushrooms, though anything can be gyoza-ified by simply wrapping it in the thin potsticker skin.

Shogayaki: Ginger pork, or shogayaki, is an easy homestyle Japanese dish that's made with thin slices of pork, ginger, and a variety of aromatics such as garlic and onion. It is served alongside rice, great for soaking up the extra gingery sauce.

Fugu : The infamous fugu pufferfish is regarded with a balance of fear and respect, but in Japan licensed chefs have mastered the art and science of preparing it, rendering the ingredient harmless. The preparation of pufferfish in Japan is extremely well-regulated, so only qualified chefs may serve it. It is often prepared as paper-thin sashimi, fried as fugu karaage, or cooked in a stew.

Gyudon: The Japanese beef-and-rice bowl, gyudon, is a classic Japanese fast food that's both comforting and hearty, with several gyudon chains vying for first place in Japan (Yoshinoya, Matsuya, and Sukiya are the main players). Consisting of thin slices of beef, tender and sweet onions, and a garnish of bright-tasting benishoga (pickled red ginger) all atop a bowl of steamed white rice, gyudon is a crowd-pleaser. Gyudon is just one of many types of Japanese rice bowl dishes, aka donburi. Check out our Guide to Donburi for a list of all the tasty rice bowl combinations available in Japan.

Karaage: A staple of izakaya (Japanese gastropubs), karaage are morsels of twice-fried Japanese fried chicken. Marinated in a mixture of soy sauce, sake, and ginger, every bite of karaage is juicy and packed with flavor, while the use of potato starch in the dredge makes Japanese fried chicken extra crispy.

Oyakodon: Another donburi (rice bowl) dish like gyudon, oyakodon is a Japanese comfort food that's the perfect dish to whip up on weekdays. Literally translating to "parent and child rice bowl," oyakodon features both chicken and egg. In one pan, onions, chicken, and beaten egg are simmered in dashi (Japanese soup stock) to make a saucy topping for a bowl of steaming rice.

Robatayaki: Craving a theatrical meal? Robatayaki or "fireside cooking" is the perfect Japanese dining experience for you. This style of cooking originated post-WWII among the fishing communities in Hokkaido and Miyagi in northern Japan, before gas became a common cooking medium. The food (often seafood) is cooked over binchotan (white charcoal), which imparts a lovely smoky flavor; and the finished dishes are passed to diners on a long wooden paddle.

Shirasu / Shirasudon : A type of seafood that's popular in Tokyo's neighboring Kanagawa prefecture, shirasu are immature whitebait fishes that are served either raw or flash-boiled. These tiny little whitebait fish may look intimidating, but we demystify this staple Japanese ingredient (and provide some tasty ways to eat shirasu) in our post, What is Shirasu? Recipes for the Entire School of Fish in Your Rice Bowl.

Somen: A traditional Japanese food that's a favorite during the sweltering and humid summertime, somen are extremely thin (think vermicelli) wheat flour noodles. Somen is enjoyed chilled, with a side of dipping sauce, often mentsuyu (a soup base made with soy sauce, mirin, sake, and dashi).For a fun summertime tradition, nagashi somen is served by channeling the noodles down a bamboo chute flowing with water, where eager diners await with their chopsticks to snatch up a mouthful of the noodles.

Imagawayaki : Imagawayaki is a traditional Japanese food, often found at festivals or food stalls outside of temples and shrines. It's a round, cake-like dessert that's filled with red bean paste or custard. A perfect portable snack, they're great for a quick bite.

Melonpan: The name melonpan (melon bread) can be a little deceiving, as these buns are designed to resemble the fruit, not necessarily taste like it. A fluffy bread with a sugar-cookie-like topping that's cross-hatched to resemble a melon, these buns come in different flavors like hojicha (roasted tea) and sweet potato. You can even find variations with ice cream!

Warabimochi : While it has "mochi" in the name, warabimochi is not, in fact, made with rice, but instead with bracken starch (warabiko). It has a jiggly texture that's more akin to jelly than a chewy mochi, and is dusted in kinako (roasted soybean powder) and drizzled with kuromitsu (black sugar syrup). A perfect Japanese wagashi for summertime, warabimochi is a refreshing sweet treat.

Tamagoyaki : The sweet-and-savory Japanese rolled omelet is another traditional Japanese food you can't miss! It's a staple in bento lunch boxes and at breakfast in Japan, a fluffy golden pillow that's made of many layers of egg wrapped around itself, and sliced into bite-sized pieces. Every family makes tamagoyaki slightly differently, and you might find it on the sweeter or savory side depending on the chef's preferences.

Tsukemono: The classic ichijiu-sansai Japanese meal layout that consists of one soup and three side dishes, would not be complete without tsukemono, or "pickled things." Japanese pickles are an indispensable part of Japanese cuisine and are served during just about every meal in Japan, in some form or other. From umeboshi (pickled plums) to takuan (pickled daikon) to benishoga (pickled red ginger), tsukemono provide an extra zing to any meal, acting as a refreshing pick-me-up in between bites.

Yokan: A traditional Japanese food that falls under the category of sweets, yokan is as classic as it gets. The history of yokan goes back centuries, coming to Japan sometime during the Kamakura or Muromachi periods. It is made of sweet red bean paste, the gelatinous agar-agar, and sugar, and is packaged in blocks that can be cut and served in bite-sized pieces alongside a cup of tea. Yokan is very sweet and very dense, so just a couple of bites will leave you satisfied.

Gyutan: Sendai in Miyagi prefecture is the proud home of gyutan, thin slices of beef tongue cooked over hot charcoals. It originally was flavored with just a pinch of salt, but these days you can get it with tare sauce.

Chankonabe: The fuel of sumo wrestlers, chankonabe is an immense stew of protein and veggies that's designed to help pack on the pounds. The hot pot is often made with a dashi or chicken soup base, and whatever proteins and vegetables are available. The main criteria for chankonabe (or "sumo stew") is that it must be hearty, served with a side of rice and beer to increase the calories. Finally, when just the broth is left, udon noodles can be added to sop up all the flavorful goodness.

Anmitsu : A classic Japanese summertime dessert, anmitsu is made with sweet red bean paste, cubes of kanten jelly, fruits, and dango. Just before eating, drizzle it with the mitsu dark sugar syrup and dig in! There are several variations of this dish, including versions with ice cream.

Hiyashi Chuka : In the mood for noodles, but too hot for ramen? Hiyashi chuka, chilled Chinese-style noodles, are the answer. The bouncy ramen noodles are topped with matchstick-size slices of cucumber, ham, and omelet, as well as other ingredients like bean sprouts and tomato, then drizzled with a dressing. The veggies provide a refreshing crunch, and the chilled noodles are satisfyingly slurpable, coated in a tangy sauce.

Kushiage: Kushiage (a.k.a. kushikatsu), are battered, deep-fried skewers of meat and vegetables. While their hometown is considered to be Osaka (play the video to watch Shizuka try these skewers for herself!), this soul food is available at eateries and izakayas across Japan; and it's no wonder–fried foods are universally-loved.

Yatsuhashi: If you've ever been to Kyoto, you've likely come across some form of yatsuhashi. A popular souvenir from Japan's ancient capital, yatsuhashi comes in two main varieties: the half-cylindrical hard-baked cinnamon-cookie type, and the "raw" yatsuhashi that's made with steamed mochi that's flattened and wrapped around an anko filling.

CHAPTER SIXTEEN

Dawat E Bengal

Architectural influences from different eras continue to be a part of the region. There are buildings of public and private use that show influences of Terracotta, Indo- Saracenic, Islam and British. The city of Calcutta used to be the Capital of India during the British reign and so it has a lot of buildings reflecting the British culture. There are various temples, mosques, churches, rajbaris (Home of the aristocratic people in the olden times).Calcutta was once known as the 'City of Palaces'. With the growing status as a cosmopolitan, Kolkata has flats coming up in its newer region.

A large part of the Bengali culture is about its cuisine. What is known as the 'Bengali food' today is a result of centuries of experiments with the ingredients coming from across the world. Numerous Kings, Zamindars, Nawabs & British officers are as responsible for the food-first culture in Bengal as the village sweet maker. Seldom in the world, would one see such democratization and acceptance for all sorts of food. Bengalis often claim that their cuisine hosts one of the most diverse palettes in South Asia. This article explores the depths of it.

Bengal and its culture teach the richness of its heritage and culture. It could be easily said that food is one of the most important things for Bengali's.

Food is an important factor as it carries the traditional norms and creative queues. Bengal's food is the pride of the state as it has huge variety to offer. When it comes to festivities and events food is the main focal point for the people, for the culture. This is because the practice of multi-cropping is quite common in Bengal which has earned fame for producing varied and good quality rice. A variety of vegetables and fruits are grown here round the year. West Bengal has a huge coastline with over sixty rivers flowing in and out of it with major rivers are like Ganges, Hoogly, Ajay, Jalangi, Damodar, Teesta, Rupnarayan, Mahananda and more. This state has a lake and pond as part of its culture and heritage that offer the populace a wide variety of fish like Ruhi, Katla, Pabda, Tangra, Koi and many more. Traditionally ghee and mustered oil are used for cooking, however, the former is now been replaced by refined oil for more modern and health-conscious Bengalis. Ghee still finds a place because it is well served with hot rice. Thus the products cultivated and found regionally dominate the food platter of a Bengali.

If we deep dive into the food and culture fish is traditionally the king of Bengali food. Rohu, Catla , and Prawns are the three most important fish along with Hilsa. It is grown in abundance between Bangladesh and West Bengal and the fish trade in this region is common. These three fishes are commonly found in the market on daily basis because they stand for staple everyday food items in a Bengali household. These days one also observes Rohu fish online availability in different parts of India where the Bengalis reside. The preparation for these fishes has a lot of variety like Rohu Curry, Katla Kalia and Prawn Malai Curry. Fish-eating habit for a Bengali's with proper quotient of taste is of top notch. Food culture has a prominence place for items like Chicken Curry or Kasha, Mutton Jhol, and some traditional Bengali dishes which are only made in Bengal.

The panch phoron most popular in Bengali cuisine includes spices like cumin, nigella, fenugreek, aniseed and mustard seed. Sukto (a bitter preparation of bitter gourd, brinjal, sweet potato and plantain); ghonto (vegetables, with or without fish, cooked in milk); jhol; ambole (sweet and sour dish of fruit, vegetables or fish) and pitha (cakes of rice flour or sweet potato fried in syrup) are some of the delicacies that form part of this cuisine.

Femous Food

- Aloo Potol Posto: Make a mental note, Bengalis love poppy seeds. They really do and why won't they, it makes food so much tastier! This preparation above is also made of poppy or Posto as the Bengalis like to call it. It is a preparation of Posto with potatoes and pointed gourd, complete with red and green chillies and sometimes coconut puree to add some much-needed spice to it. It truly is one of the classic Bengali dishes and famous food of West Bengal!
- Jhal Muri – Spicy Puffed Rice Salad Jhal muri is trendy Bengali chaat or fresh salad that is spicy, chatpata and made of puffed rice.

- Ilish Macher Jhol: One of the much-favoured fishes in the region, Hilsa or ilish fish curry is something that you have got to try your hands on. The pungent smelling curry prepared with Nigella seeds and chilli to give it the required balance that makes it so perfect. You have got to try this one as it one of the staple food of West Bengal.
- Shukto: Who said Bengalis are all for fish and nothing else? Well, Bengalis do know how to do their vegetables too. And Shukto is just an example. Usually served as the first course of a diet, Shukto is a combination of different vegetables like Brinjals, Bitter Gourd, Crunchy Drumsticks and Bori (a Bengali speciality again). Mixed with grounded spices and milk to make a thick curry, this is a perfect way to start a meal.
- Sandesh: The most popular sweet from the Bengali state, this dish is made of khoya, a version of condensed milk and is heavenly in taste. This sweet is neither overly sweet thus allowing people with a non-sweet tooth to enjoy too. One should definitely try this delectable West Bengal food item.
- Chutney: West Bengal is notable for its chutney, setting a separate course aside for this sweet and sticky dish. There are many different kinds of chutney, and the sweetness provided by the condiment is a precursor to the final dessert course of the meal. The often experimental use of different fruits to create the sweet and pungent flavors of chutney have been adopted and appropriated worldwide, but many of the best types are to be found within Bengal. Popular variants are made using mango, papaya, pineapple and tomatoes, and the dish is eaten alongside papadums.
- Plastic Chutney: As weird as plastic chutney sounds, it is one of the most famous chutneys in Bengal. Bengali Plastic Chutney is nothing more than raw papaya chutney that looks like melted plastic. If you are thinking, why is this dish called a plastic chutney? Then it's only because of the glossy translucent texture the papaya gets after being dipped in sugar. To make this chutney all you need to do is cut your papaya into thin pieces. After that take a wok and mix salt, sugar and water in it. When they combine, throw in your thin papaya slices and let it cook for 10 minutes on low heat. Make this easily at home and pair it with any food that you like!
- Tomato-Khajur Chutney: Tomato, cranberry, and dates are used to make the Bengali Style Tomato Khajur Chutney. This Chutney is a simple side dish made with flavours that are sweet, sour, and tangy. This Chutney

will tingle the sense of taste. This one Chutney is especially common for Bengalis because it is a prevalent flavor in their dishes.

- Red Pumpkin Chutney: Many have not heard about this Chutney, but once you get your hands on this one, it makes a delicious affair to have with all kinds of food. The cooked and mashed red pumpkin is mixed with spices like chillis, tamarind, raisins, which gives it both sweet and savoury flavour. If you are serving hot crunchy snacks, this chutney could be the perfect side dish.
- Apple Chutney: While this may not be that popular, the Bengal apple chutney certainly holds its name among Bengalis. This sweet and sour Chutney is easy to make at home, so if you have any leftover apple, mash it up and put it in the pan to make this tangy Chutney.
- Kasundi: Kasundi is traditional Bengali chutney that goes well with snacks, light meals, and appetizers. This delicious plate, also known as Bengal Mustard Sauce, is made with tomato, mustard seeds, white vinegar, cayenne pepper, and garlic. During the monsoon season, serve this simple recipe with your favourite fritters and immerse yourself in the world of spicy flavours. One of the benefits of making this delicious recipe is that it could be stored for days.
- Posto Bata: Made with the goodness of poppy seeds hand ground with freshly grated coconut, this simple condiment is often relished with steamed rice and green chilies. Poppy seeds also known as Khas khas is known for its amazing cooling as well as sleep inducing properties, which makes it a perfect summer treat!
- Aam er Tok: Made with raw mangoes, this sweet and tangy delight is perfect for the changing season. To make this easy chutney, you need 250 grams of raw mangoes, washed and peeled. Chop the mangoes into small cubes and soak them in water to remove the excessive astringent taste. Then take a pan and add 1 ½ tablespoon of mustard oil, add in some mustard seeds along with two whole dried red chilies broken, toss these for a minute or so. Next, add the chopped mangoes and toss them nicely, add some salt and turmeric powder. Then add in around 350 ml water along with ½ cup sugar. You can adjust the water and sugar as per your taste and lastly add a dash of red chile powder and cover the lid and let the chutney simmer.
- Kacha Kola Bata: Made with the goodness of raw banana peels, this delicacy helps in keeping the system calm during the changing weather. To make this quick paste, wash and pressure cook the peel of 2 bananas.

Once the peel is cooked nicely, then take a blender and add 3 green chilies, 5-6 garlic cloves, 1inch ginger and salt as per taste. To make the tempering, take a pan and add 1 tablespoon of mustard oil, add some nigella seeds, 2 red chilies whole let it splutter and pour it over the paste mix and serve hot with steamed rice.

- Payesh (Kheer): This rice pudding dish is made using glutinous rice, milk and sugar. The sweetness is further enhanced by adding nuts such as almonds, cashews or pistachios, or dried fruits, cardamom and saffron for more luxurious versions. The dish is commonly seen prepared in temples, and in eastern India is consumed at special celebrations such as birthdays. In Bangladesh, the dish is made slightly differently, using coconut milk and semolina, which makes for a more glutinous, sweeter pudding
- Mutton Biryani: Although made famous in various parts of the country, each marked with unique cooking techniques and spices; one should also try this taste in this part of the country. Filled with the rich aroma of spices and ghee, the mutton biryani is simply heaven. Juicy, tender pieces of mutton, fried with the biryani on a Tava, this yummy recipe is a must-try.
- Aam Pora Shorbot: A drink made of chilled water, burnt raw mangoes and sugar, it is an instant relief that you will get on a sweltering summer afternoon (and with the Kolkata heat you might as well require it). The raw mangoes are burnt, but only partially, with the skin a bit charred which lends a smoky taste to the drink. Best served chilled; this drink is surely the one which is more relaxing and refreshing than the colas with artificial sweetness.
- Bengali Mutton Curry (Kosha Mangsho): It is about Mutton Kawsha of the last century famously reputed 'kasha mangsho', one of the signature dish of Kolkata, first presented commercially by the New Punjabi Hotel popular as "Golbari" situated at Shyambazar five points established by late Ratan Arora around 1915-1920 still available the original dish there with
- Tangra Macher Jhol: As you are familiar with the fact that Bengal has a rich source of fresh water as well as saltwater fishes, you might also know the fact that Bengal tries a lot of different varieties of fishes. The Tangra fish is basically the catfish that is found in the freshwater bodies abound in the region. The fish is prepared with freshly ground spices, and the thin curry is light on the stomach and also supremely tasty too.

It is a big hit among the Bengalis in the region.

- Alur Dom: Although there are different ways to prepare this dish made of potatoes, it continues to be a hit in the regular Bengali household. If there is nothing else in the house, potatoes always come to the rescue. The dish can be incorporated with many different spices and prepared in many different ways. It is most commonly eaten with Luchi, another Bengali delicacy.
- Begun Bhaja (Brinjal Fry): A simple yet spicy marinade of chili powder, turmeric, and lime seasoned with salt and pan-fried with mustard oil. Baja refers to frying and can be a variety of vegetables or meat fried. Eggplant, or aubergine, is a favorite among Bengalis. Coat the eggplant with rice flour to get a crispy outside and moist inside. Potatoes, pumpkin, bitter gourd, onions, and green plantains can be used in place of eggplant. Usually served as an appetizer, this dish is a quick and easy way to satisfy hungry bellies any time of the day.
- Dhokar Dalna (Lentil Cake Curry): Dhokar refers to split chickpeas that are ground and formed into cakes and steeped in a thick curry with cubed potatoes, cumin seeds, hing, and bay leaf along with ginger and red chili paste. This is a star among the veggie dishes that make up traditional Bengali cuisine and is reserved usually for special occasions like religious festivals and days of abstinence, when meat or fish isn't consumed. It is best served with steamed white rice. The name is derived from the word dhoka, which means betrayal, referring to the meat-like consistency and texture of the chickpea cakes, something along the lines of mock meat. The base of the gravy is usually made with satvik ingredients. Satvik refers to the omission of onions and garlic and it is a cuisine that is popular within the Jain community in India and also followed by certain Hindu castes.
- Luchi: A deep-fry delicacy, no Bengali household can ever complete a celebration without Luchis. Prepared with maida instead of the atta flour which is used to make chapattis, this delicacy looks like smaller sized, fluffy, deep-fried chapattis, with a golden glow. The crispy Luchis are a mandate for all the important small celebrations that take place in the Bengali household.
- Chholar Dal: One of the Bengali's favourite dals, this dish is made with chana dal as the main ingredient. With its slightly sweet and spicy taste, the dal is perfect to eat with rice or Luchis. Addition of delicious spices like bay leaves, coconut bits and cinnamon increases the taste manifold.

Although one may get a lot of gourmet dishes, the real Bengali taste is in the simple dishes prepared in the common Bengali household.

- Lau Ghonto: Lau is bottle gourd, which is cooked with Udad Dal Boris and some light spices. Although the dish is not so spicy, it is good for the stomach and delicious too, so that is a bonus. Try this recipe if you want to rest your stomach after a hard day at work. Enjoy this Bengali food with rice.
- Mochar Ghonto: Mochar Ghonto is a delicious preparation of banana flower, crushed coconut and potato, cooked with some cumin and bay leaves. This mouth-watering dish is filled with the sweetness and spice that makes it an amazing try. An authentic Vegetarian west Bengal dish, this is proof that there is more to Bengalis than fish and meat.
- Kosha Mangsho: This dish of mutton with some thick curry is high on spices and richness. This dish is made with mutton and spices such as cloves, cinnamon, onion and garlic are used. This excellent recipe is full of the aroma and sweetness that is surely going to trigger your taste buds.
- Bhetki Paturi: Paturi recipe is a special way of cooking which we can apply for any fish, but here we will discover the steps to prepare Bhetki fish paturi recipe at home. In Bengal we prepare mostly Bhetki paturi or hilsha paturi. If you are a vegetarian, then go ahead and try this with paneer or with some other vegetables. You will definitely enjoy the preparation as well the food
- Joynagar-er Moya: Joynagarer moa is a seasonal Bengali sweetmeat delicacy prepared from date palm jaggery and puffed rice. This variety of moa originated in Joynagar, West Bengal, India. It is now a popular sweet, being produced in Kolkata and elsewhere, sometimes with cheaper ingredients and chemical flavours
- Chingri Maacher Malaikari: Golda Chingri or SCAMPI cooked in coconut milk is a traditional Bengali dish and usually part of the menu of formal Bengali lunch. The most subtle of all is the Golda Chingri Malaikari, a cuisine from Bengali speaking people in India.
- Bhapa Ilish: This recipe has been adopted from Bangladesh. In this recipe raw Ilish/Hilsha pieces are steamed in mustard along with turmeric, green chili, salt, mustard oil. This is an effortless cooking. Only marinate the fish and put into a non-stick pan and cook on low heat for 20-30 minutes. No need to stir or add something in
- Bardhaman-er Langcha

  Langcha is a famous sweet of West Bengal. This is one of those popular fried sweets that India is famous for. Shaktigarh in the Bardhaman District of West Bengal is famous for this sweet item. Langcha is one of the most delicious Bengali Sweets.

- Krishnanagar-er Sarbhaja: Yes, it is true that Bengalis are inseparable from sweets. Bengali sweets are famous for its unforgettable taste and innovativeness. In spite of having such a wide variety of sweets we treasure a special love for the traditional sweets which are not easily available these days.
- Lau Patai Pabda Paturi (Steamed Pabda Fish in Bottled Gourd Leaf): Pabda refers to the Indian catfish that is found in abundance across the Mangroves of the Sunderbans. It is not an extremely bony fish, having one main bone running through the length of the body. Pabda Macher Kalo Jeerer Jhol is cooked light with minimal spices. The flavors of fresh coriander mustard and chilies are an absolutely mouth-watering combination. This dish is best served with rotis or parathas.
- Macher Matha Diye Moong Dal: An unlikely combination of lentils and fried fish head, this is a delicacy reserved for a traditional Bengali table. The flavor of fresh carp head fried and infused with roasted moong dal is an absolute treat for the senses. There is no other dal in Bengali cuisine that occupies a higher position than this dish.
- Shorshe Ilish: A popular dish from the wetlands of Bengal, stretching across borders between India and Bangladesh, this humble yet flavorful dish unites two favorites of the region: hilsa or Tenualosa ilisha, a type of herring found in the rivers and tributaries that span the region, and mustard seeds. the fish is mainly found, and in the neighboring Indian states of West Bengal, Tripura, and Assam's Barak valley. Hilsa, white mustard, mustard oil, green chili, black cumin, turmeric powder, red chili powder, and salt are the main ingredients. Lime juice and/or coriander leaves may also be added for flavor.
- Ilish Paturi (Hilsa Cooked in Banana Leaf): Ilish Macher Paturi combines three of Bengal's greatest loves – the Hilsa fish, the banana plant, and mustard. Even though it looks very polished, it is a fairly easy recipe to execute. It requires very few ingredients, no special technique, and can be cooked very quickly. This simple recipe calls for a smooth marinade of mustard seeds, ginger, and turmeric, which is blended with mustard oil and beaten yogurt. The fish is then coated with this marinade and wrapped in banana leaves and then cooked over a hot griddle with a little bit of oil. A visually appetizing masterpiece for any dinner table. Best

served with basmati rice.

- Aam Tel Ilish (Mango-flavored Hilsa Steamed in Pumpkin Leaf): Aam Tel Ilish which is mango pickle-flavored, steamed boneless Hilsa wrapped in a pumpkin leaf and served in a clay pot with steamed rice – a favorite at Oh Calcutta, Bengaluru's best Bengali restaurant. Mustard fresh ginger and tangy mango pickle are ground into a smooth paste. The fish is then fried and tempered in this puree along with copious amounts of mustard oil.
- Macher Chop (Bengali Fish Croquette): Calcutta being the administrative center of the British Raj in India has adopted various techniques and recipes and added their own culinary twist. This includes the Chop or Chaap, which refers to a cutlet or croquette that can be filled with potatoes, fish, or even meat.It is usually eaten as a snack or accompaniment to the main course and is a favorite for many. The bread crumb coated fish cutlet or chop is a beloved recipe, is very simple to make, and can also be done using leftovers.
- Gondhoraj Maach (Fish with Kafir Lime): Gondhoraj Ibeu, locally called the Rangpur lime, is a variety of lime indigenous to Bengal. It is surprising how understated it is, given its culinary prowess. Just a few drops are enough to elevate the most humble and insipid dishes into divine delectable masterpieces. The canton lime from China, hime from Japan, and the famous key lime from the Florida Keys and Caribbean would be close competitors of the wonderful olfactory experience this provides. The barramundi or Asian sea bass is the preferred fish here, for its boneless and soft texture, paired with a mild sauce flavored with cream, yogurt, and a ginger-chili-garlic paste. The icing on the cake of course being the Godhoraj lime juice and zest to finish it off.
- Calcutta Fish Fry: Calcutta's very own batter-fried fish is inspiration from the yesteryear of the British Raj. It is a street food novelty and beloved by the locals of the city. Various fish can be used, such as vetki, barramundi, tilapia, cod, swai, and basa. Onions, ginger, garlic, green chili, coriander, and mint are ground into a fine paste, which is then coated over the fish fillets. Lemon juice and pepper can also be added. After an egg wash, the fillets are coated in bread crumbs and deep-fried to perfection. Served with the local kashundi or mustard and mango sauce or tomato ketchup, it is a treat for the senses on a cold monsoon evening on the streets of Calcutta.

- Chingri Pulao (Prawn Pilaf): A specialty reserved for "Noboborsho" or Bengali New Year, this is a simple yet flavorful dish and an attractive way to serve your guests a delectable rice preparation. It is something different from the traditional biryani. It can be prepared in one pot and is a quick fix in a tight situation. Fennel, cumin, cardamom, cinnamon, mace, and nutmeg are some of the common spices used in this dish, with whole spices preferred over ground powders. Large to medium-sized prawns are cooked with the spices and the rice is added and steamed together.
- Bengali Mishti Pulao (Cashew & Raisin Pilaf): Bengal is famous for its variety of sweets made with milk, milk fudge, and cheese. Just as famous as the sweet Misthi Pulao, Basmati is the choice of rice. The pulao is flavored with green cardamom, bay leaf, and cloves. The addition of ghee or clarified butter transforms the dish from a mundane rice preparation into an ornate addition to your dining table. Finally, a little sugar, roasted cashew nuts, and raisins are added before it is steamed to perfection. Best served with a spicy curry or meat, this dish with its light flavors and richness is ideal for cutting through the sharpness of a spicy hearty meat dish.
- Macher Jhol (Bengali Fish Curry): Bengal and especially Kolkatta, being situated on one of the largest delta basins and mangrove coasts in the world, enjoys a bountiful supply of seafood, freshwater, and seawater fish. But there is one fish that is especially close to the heart of every Bengali: the infamous Hilsa or Ilish.
- Postor Bora: Postor bora is a mix of poppy seed paste, grated coconut, onions, green chilies, and rice flour, which are shallow fried as fritters in mustard oil. It is an absolute delicacy for Bengalis and is known for its extraordinary flavor and texture. It is the perfect fritter, with the outer crisp containing of poppy seeds and a tender center. It is mostly served as a starter or as a side with the main course to relish. Posto bora is a very simple and easy recipe and requires very minimal and easily available ingredients. The best part of the recipe is that it requires very little oil, unlike other bora (pakoda). It can be prepared very easily without too much time and you it can be prepared in batches. So it is a great option for any get-together and small party.
- Keemar Doi Bora: West Bengal is certainly a paradise for non-vegetarians. A paradigmatic minced meat preparation holds the cultural connection with the family of Nobel Laureate Rabindra Nath Tagore.

Keemar Doi Bora was introduced by Purnima Thakur when she discovered the Tagore family cookbook. An invention of the Thakurbari, Keemar Doi Bora are fried meatballs in sweet and spiced curd that is a twist to the usual Dahi vada. Bengalis' usually make these balls with mutton or chicken keema. However, for a vegetarian, it can also be made with soya granules. It is a perfect snack for any occasion.

- Kolar Bora: The popular snack, Kolar Bora are banana fritters known to be the favorites of Lord Krishna. Soft from inside and crunchy from outside, these banana fritters or pakoras are the best tea time munching snacks. This Bong dessert is a must during Janmashtami and Makar Sankranti.
- Bardhaman-er Sitabhog: This is actually a Bengali Special Dish called Sita-Bhog. A myth about this sweet's name is that this Sweet is one of the favorite sweet of Mata Sita. Mainly this recipe is famous in Bardhaman, a district of West Bengal. But Nowadays in West Bengal including Kolkata at each and every sweets shop you will find it.
- Mishti Doi: Mishti Doi is a sweetened yoghurt dish that is served at the end of supper and serves as a sweet dish. Though served all around the country now, it was initially made famous by Bengal. Try it if you have a sweet tooth.
- Patishapta: Another unique Bengali sweet, this is usually homemade with a batter of powdered rice and rolled with the preparation of coconut bits with sugar and khoya. One of the most amazing Bengali dishes, one has got to try this one, sweet tooth or not. I am sure you are going to love it.
- Lobong Lotika: Shaped to resemble a tiny envelope, which is then sealed with a single clove, the Lobongo Lotika is usually savoured during special occasions, but who's looking anyway? Made with refined flour pastry, stuffed with a mix of khoya, grated coconut, nuts, raisins, and cardamom, which is then folded like an envelope, held together with a stick of clove, it is then fried in ghee, and soaked in thick sugar syrup for a little while to make it extra, how shall we put it, sinful
- Kheer Kadam: I am a Kheer Kadam monster. I will eat my share, and yours too. Named after the Kadamba (a ball-shaped flower with tiny white petals that point in all directions), this sweetmeat is made by encasing a dry Rasgulla (smaller than the usual one), coated first with kheer, which is then dusted with dried kheer. The idea is to bite into the shell, and then let the Rasgulla take over. Ideally pop the whole thing into

your mouth and relish it.

- Patishapta: This stuffed pancake roll is preserved for Makar Sankranti, and is always made at home. Stuffed with a coconut and jaggery mix, it's typically had warm because the filling doesn't quite do the trick otherwise. The pancake batter is made with maida (all purpose flour), semolina, and rice flour, and is mixed with milk. And it has to be really thin too. In many homes, the filling is made with sugar instead of jaggery, which isn't my favourite kind. Some even drizzle a bit of sweet thickened milk on top of the roll before serving.
- Chhanar Jilipi: Fat, soft, and exceedingly decadent – the Chhanar Jilipi is made with chhana (cottage cheese), khoya, and maida. It's deep fried, and then soaked in sugar syrup (flavoured with cardamom).
- Shor Bhaja: The Shor Bhaja (directly translated from fried milk cream) is probably one of the toughest sweets to make. And it's not because of the recipe, but the labour that goes into it. Typically it should involve nothing but layers of milk cream, deep fried and soaked in sugar syrup. But there are certain variations that include the adding of cardamom and rose water for flavour and essence.
- Pantua: This is NOT a Gulab Jamun, as most people might claim. Made with chhana, maida, semolina, ghee, and sugar, it is deep fried and soaked in sugar syrup. A perfect golden brown Pantua will be slightly spongy (not as much as the Rasgulla), with some of the juice oozing out as you bite into it. This one can be served hot, or even cold.
- Joynogorer Moa: Made with date palm jaggery (nolen gur that's suddenly become a star ingredient in many restaurants across India), puffed rice from a special fragrant rice called Kanakchur, pure ghee, cardamom, and poppy seeds, it's particularly available in winter because both the puffed rice and the jaggery belong to that season. It is shaped to form round balls, and usually topped with a raisin or two. The authentic moa is never hard or dry, and ideally shouldn't even crumble on bite, even though it looks like it would. This is where the jaggery comes handy, delicately holding the puffed rice in place.
- Ladikeni: Made with chhana, semolina, ghee, granulated sugar and raisins, it's shaped into oblongs, and deep fried in ghee. It is then soaked in sugar syrup flavoured with cardamom and saffron strands.
- Joynogor-er Moa: Moa is a delicious dry concoction made out of jaggery, puffed rice and ghee that is packed together into a round delicious ball. We recommend the seasonally available Joynagar-er Moa which is

perhaps one of the tastiest Bengali sweets you will ever try. This specific type is also dotted with dry fruits and nuts. Moa can be made with 'muri' or 'Khoi'.

- Chandrapuli: Shaped like a pale crescent moon, this dessert is made from cottage cheese, mawa, coconut and jaggery. Because of the combination of ingredients, this can be the perfect dessert to indulge your sweet tooth. Be warned, however, that for some it may be a little too sweet. A popular Bengali sweet, it is enjoyed during festive occasions such as Durga Puja.

CHAPTER SEVENTEEN

Kathiyawadi Food Festival

Kathiyawadi cuisine – a spicy and fiery cuisine that hails from an Indian western state Gujarat. Kathyiawad is comprised of Saurashtra region with major cities such as Porbandar, Jamnagar, Bhavnagar, Rajkot and Junagadh. It is one of the oldest cuisines of India that is gaining popularity for a wholesome, fresh meal made with simple ingredients that are readily available.

Kathiawar or Saurashtra hosts a large number of communities, castes and settlements in the region, though the Kathis after whom the name of Kathiawar became popular is a distinct group. Often in everyday conversation, a person from Kathiawar is called a "Kathiawadi".

Kathiawad is a peninsula in western India, which is part of the Saurashtra region on the Arabian Sea coast of Gujarat state. It is bounded on the north by the great wetland of the Rann of Kutch..It is surprising to know that Saurashtra with its vast stretches of dry earth has sugarcane, wheat, millet, peanuts, and sesame native to this region. Gujarati , specially kathiwari food is notably dry due to geographical location, and lack of water resources. Hence pulses (gram flour) dominate Kathiawari food and sweetmeats made of gur (jaggery). Onion, potato and garlic are used widely in combination of dairy products as these are a substitute of green leafy vegetables that cannot be grown in harsh dry climate around the year. The cuisine changes with the seasonal availability of vegetables.The wide variety of taste by Gujarati, ranging from extreme sweet items like peda, jalebi to extreme spicy taste like pickles and chutneys. Many Gujarati dishes are distinctively sweet, salty, and spicy at the same time. A Gujarati thali can not be complete without staples like Garlic chutney, raw onions, chilli pickle- or fried green chilies, Chaas (Butter milk), papad, and ghee with jaggaery.

Kathiyawadi Delicacies:

Ringan no Oro: A spicy, hot and tangy dish made with aubergine. Chargrilled aubergines mashed and cooked with fresh tomatoes and spices.

Bateta nu Shaak: In Gujarati, it is literally translated as Potato Curry. This is a saucy dish that pairs well with fulka roti (the paper thin chapati).

Dal dhokli – First, tempered pigeon pea dal is prepared. Then a wheat flour-based flat bread is rolled, cut into diamond-shaped pieces and immersed within the dal itself. This delectable, yet simple, dish is served with pure ghee to make it even more indulgent.

Lasaniya Bateta: Lasaniya means garlic and Bateta means potato. This is a spicy hot garlic flavoured potatoes cooked with onion, tomato and spices.

Vagharelo Rotlo: Shredded flatbread cooked with buttermilk and seasoned with spices. This is a great way to turn leftover flatbread to a delicious and wholesome new dish.

Undiyu: One-pot mixed vegetable casserole cooked in a clay pot. A pot filled with vegetables, spices is buried underground in a large furnace covered by a pile of dried leaves and are set alight to cook. Traditionally this dish is cooked upside down and the name comes from the Gujarati term “Undhu” which means upside down.

Vaghareli Khichdi: The most aromatic and comfort dish from Kathiyawadi cuisine. “Vaghareli” translates to seasoning where rice and lentils are cooked and seasoned with spices and vegetables

Bajra no Rotlo: A plain flatbread made with pearl millet flour. This healthy and nutritious millet bread makes a good option for lunch and dinner.

Kaju Karela: Crunchy and delicious bitter gourd stir-fry. Bitter gourd slices are tossed with jaggery, poppy seeds, cashews and spices.

Kadhi – Gujarati for curry, it is typically made with buttermilk, gram flour and sugar, which is tempered and flavoured with ginger and chilli. A slightly sweet curry, Gujaratis are known to add radish and even bananas to make this dish more flavourful.

Bateta Vada: A popular potato fritters served as a tea-time snack or an appetiser. A mashed potato balls battered with gram flour and deep fried until crisp.

Guvar Dhokli nu Shaak: A main course dish made with flour dumplings and cluster beans.

Methi Thepla: A simple and versatile flatbread made with wheat flour and fenugreek leaves. This soft flatbread makes a perfect breakfast, evening snack or for dinner.

Shrikhand – Made of hung curd and sugar, this dairy-based dessert is soft and light, and served cold. It may also contain dry fruits, saffron or cardamom powder for added flavour.

Adadiya Pak: A traditional Kathiyawadi dessert prepared with ingredients that helps to keep body warm on cold winter days.

Muthiya – This dish is a combination of wheat flour and pearl millet or gram flour, which is mixed with cooked rice, rolled and then steamed. It can be made with methi leaves and doodhi as well.

Gathiya – A type of savoury snack made of gram flour and masalas, gathiya is also a type of sev and comes in various shapes and sizes. Gathiya is either eaten on its own or taken with tea.

Fafda – A type of gathiya that is long, flat and has a salty taste topped with asafoetida. It makes for a great combination with the sweet jalebi.

Khakhra – Wheat flour flat breads are dry roasted until crispy and then topped with ghee and a spicy masala.

Chakri – Made with rice flour, which is mixed with ginger, chilli and sesame seeds. The chakri is shaped in a spiral and deep-fried. Another dish that is commonly consumed as a snack.

Patra – Arbi patta (colocasia leaves) are lathered with a paste made of gram flour, jaggery, garam masala, sesame seeds, and tamarind. These leaves are then rolled and steamed. Patra is typically served as an appetiser.

Basundi – Thick boiled milk mixed with sugar and saffron. Served cold.

Puran Pori: A jaggery-lentil stuffed flatbread that makes a perfect after meal dish.

Pickles (Athanu): As with any Indian cuisine, pickles are an integral part of Gujarati food culture as well. The most popular pickle in Gujarat is undoubtedly goonda-keri (cordia and unripe mango). It is a piquant pickle made with a mix of spices known as methiya masala. Another favoured athanu is the chundo, which is a yummy sweet and sour pickle. It is also prepared with unripe grated mangoes. Sugar is an important element in chundo as well. Lastly, there is god-keri, which involves the use of unripe mangoes with jaggery to form a sweet and sour pickle.

CHAPTER EIGHTEEN

Awadhi Food Festival

The Awadhi cuisine attained its distinctive flavour under the patronage of the Nawabs of Awadh. Burhan-ul-Mulk Saadat Khan, the first Nawab, was of Persian origin. Thus, Persian cultural practices became an intrinsic part of the courtly culture under the Nawabs. The culinary culture was no exception. The cuisine that was perfected in the royal kitchens of the Nawabs was a harmonious blend of Mughal, Persian and local influences. The most distinctive feature of the Awadhi cuisine is the careful blend of spices used. Many a time, Awadhi food is confused with Mughlai food. Although Awadhi style of cooking has drawn considerably from Mughal cuisine, there are important differences between the two. One of the most important differences that make Awadhi food distinct from Mughlai food is that while the latter is marked by a zealous use of spices, nuts, milk and cream, the former is known for its subtle and delicate flavours and nuanced use of spices.

The desire for achieving a unique style is reflected in the dumpukht style of preparation, which is considered to be the hallmark of Awadhi cooking. It is believed that the dumpukht style has its origins in the cooking techniques of Persia and Central Asia. This method usually involves cooking in a heavy-bottomed vessel with its lid sealed (with dough) and left over a low fire for several hours, sometimes even overnight, to cook. The word dum means to breathe in and pukht means to cook. Thus, the technique of dumpukht means letting the food breathe in its own aroma or juices and also become deeply infused with the flavour of the accompanying spices. Gile hikmat is a unique technique of cooking used in Awadhi cuisine. In this technique, the meat or vegetable is stuffed with nuts and spices, wrapped in a banana leaf, covered in a layer of clay or multani mitti and buried in the earth. A low simmering fire is placed on the surface above. After letting it cook for several hours, the dish is considered ready to eat. Apart from this, other techniques like dhungar, which involved infusing a dish with the aroma of charcoal though smoking, were also used.

Spices have a prominent role to play in Awadhi cuisine. As mentioned earlier, the Awadhi dishes were crafted around a careful and harmonious blend of spices. Spices, generally popular in the Indian subcontinent such as cinnamon, peppercorn, cloves, cardamom, bay leaf, cumin, mace and nutmeg were used in the Awadhi kitchens. It is said that in the royal households, recipes were crafted and closely guarded within families of royal cooks and were passed down from one generation to another. Even today, many outlets of Awadhi food in old Lucknow, whose owners have been involved in this profession for several generations, boast of secret family recipes that make their food distinct from others. Awadhi cuisine consists of both vegetarian and non-vegetarian dishes. Some of the most celebrated dishes include kebabs, biryani, korma and nihari. Kebabs are mostly made of minced meat or vegetable bound in the shape of disks or cylindrical forms. Some of the most popular non-vegetarian kebabs are kakori, shami, galawti, boti and seekh. Vegetarian versions include kathal, arbi, matar and rajma galawti kebabs. Kebabs are accompanied by rotis or breads which could again be of various forms: rumali, tandoori, naan, kulcha, sheermal and baqarkhani.

The Awadhi Dum Biryani is a rice dish in which rice and meat are cooked separately and then layered and cooked again for several hours in a sealed vessel over a low fire. It is distinct from the other varieties of biryani found in the Indian subcontinent and is known for its subtle and delicate flavour. The qorma is a dish consisting of either meat or vegetables braised with yogurt cream, water or stock to produce a viscous sauce. Nihari is a meat-based stew that is slow-cooked till the meat melts to merge with the texture of the stew. During the time of the Nawabs, the preparation of food in the royal kitchens was an elaborate affair. The workforce in the kitchen had its own divisions. For example, the bawarchis were responsible for cooking in large numbers, for an entire household on a regular basis. The rakabdars were gourmet cooks that specialized in cooking select dishes and also in innovating to keep the royal menu interesting and updated. The nanfus were in charge of making various kinds of bread.

Another important element that defines Awadhi cuisine and the culinary culture of Nawabs is the concept of dastarkhwan. A dastarkhwan implies an elaborate ceremonial spread of dishes: qorma, salan (a thin gravy), qeema (minced meat dish), kebabs, pulao (rice flavoured with spices, distinct from biryani), a variety of rotis, desserts such as kheer (a kind of pudding), firni (another variety of pudding) and so on. Traditionally, the dishes were supposed to be eaten in a particular order. Nazakat and tehzeeb, roughly translated as 'grace' and 'manners', formed an important part of the dining process. In modern times, the term dastarkhwan has come to denote the table cloth that is spread for laying food. The presentation of a dish was also as important as its flavour. Ittr or perfume was used to enhance the aroma of food, and leaves of flattened silver and gold, called chandi warq and sona warq, were used for decorating the dishes.

Salient Features

1. In olden days, three classes of people were employed in preparing food. The scullions who cleaned enormous pots and dishes worked under bavarchi (cook), who cooked food in large quantities. The 'rakabdar', the most expert chef usually cooked food in small gourmet quantities for the nobility.

2. People living in Awadh region are basically Muslims who have a great affinity towards rich and heavy dishes, which makes Awadhi food altogether a different affair. Awadhi food is rich in spices and oils. There is more emphasis on finners of gravies (some are strained to make finer).

3. Breakfast: Generally slightly heavy as compared to other meals. The items may include stuffed parathas, sauteed offals etc.

4. Lunch: Constitutes rice, non-veg gravy, bread, a vegetable and a dessert.

5. Dinner: Traditionally starts with a Kebab, (starter) followed by normal courses.

6. The Bawairchies and Rakabdars by their expertise of blending spices achieved a high degree of finners in cooking. This gave birth to Dum style of cooking or the art of cooking over a slow flame, within sealed containers and preferably heated from the top as well (by live coal).

7. The Lucknow 'Dastarkhwan' would not be complete unless it had

8. Awadh is also famous for its pickles, murabbas, and various kinds of sweet dishes.

i. Korma : Braised meat in thick gravy.

ii. Salan: A gravy dish of meat and vegetables

iii. Kheema: Minced meat

iv. Kebabs: Pounded meat cooked over coal fire.

v. Bhujia: well cooked vegetables

vi. Dal:

9. Nahari is a hot favourite of Awadhi; and is a meat preparation with thick spicy gravy. In 'paye ki Nahari' bones are cooked and bone juices are mixed with the gravy. It is eaten traditionally with Kulchas.

10. Lucknowis have an affinity to pulao than to Biriyanis. There are some unique techniques in making Lucknowi pulaos. In 'Yakhni pulao', a thick meat broth (yakhni) is prepared in which whole spices are not added directly but wrapped and tied in a muslin cloth and dropped in to the broth. Afterwards, it is taken out. The rice is then cooked in this broth. And the vessel is sealed to retain the flavour.

11. The Lucknowi menu changes with season. The severity of winter is fought with rich food. Paya (trotters) are cooked overnight over slow fire and shorba (thick gravy) eaten with naans. Birds like partridge and quail are had since they are heat giving meats. They prefer fish usually 'rohu' (fresh water). For winter, fish Kebabs cooked in mustard oil are consumed.

12. Peas are the most sought after vegetables. Sawan (Spring) is celebrated with pakwan (wisp snacks) phulkis (besan pakoras in salan) curamba (A dessert with raw mangoes cooked in semolina and jaggery/ sugar) is eaten in summer. These dishes come from rural Hindu community.

13. Awadh is also famous for its pickles, murabbas, and various kinds of sweet dishes.

Utensils are used to cook this special form of cuisine.

- Mahi tawa are especially designed for preparing kebabs. It has a flat bottom with raised edges. It is round in shape. Mahi tawa is also used for any other food items that require heat produced from both end when covered.
- Seeni is a round tray used to cover Mahi tawa and lagan. Burning charcoal are spread on top of the tray and it acts as a lid for the utensils. Seeni is mostly used when the food requires indirect heat from all sides.
- Lagan is used to heat whole meat or large chunks of meat. It is round in shape with a shallow, concave bottom. The utensil is made of copper.
- Bhagona or patili is used for sautéing, boiling and simmering. Food items like korma, yakhni, salan, kaliya are best cooked in this brass utensil.
- Deg or degchi is ideally meant for dum style. Pulao, biriyani, nahari are best cooked in deg. The utensil is made of copper, aluminium or brass.
- Lohe ka tandoor is used for making bread items like taftan, sheermal, bakarhani. It is a dome- shaped iron oven.
- Kadhai is meant for deep frying and has a deep shallow concave bottom.

Some of their authentic cooking techniques include:

Dhungar is a technique used in Awadhi cuisine to impart the smoky flavor in the food.

How to impart smoky flavor in Awadhi curries and kormas?

The smoky flavor can be added to any Awadhi dish in three simple steps.

1) Ignite a lump of coal on the gas burner.

2) With the help of kitchen tongs, put the ignited coal inside a stainless steel katori and place it in the wok (degchi).

3) Add a tablespoon of ghee on top and cover the wok with a lid. Open after 10 minutes and serve.

Awadhi and Mughlai cuisine different from each other: Even if the flavors might be similar, Awadhi and Mughlai cuisine are very different from each other. While Mughlai cuisine uses a lot of heavy cream and milk products to bring out the flavor, Awadhi cuisine relies more on masalas and enhancing the flavor of the meat or the key ingredient used. Awadhi kebabs are slow cooked on a girdle while 'tikkas' or kebabs from other parts of the country are cooked in a tandoor.

Dastarkhwan is where people sit around and enjoy the food prepared by the bawarchis, this is the place dining spread is laid ceremonially and it is a customary to share food in Awadhi. It is said that the richness of Awadh cuisine not only lies on the variety but the type of ingredient used to make the dish.

Ghee Durust Karna : This is a process of tempering ghee with kewra water and cardamom pods so that aromatic ghee is used for various purposes.

Dhungar : A quick smoking techniques used to flavor meat dishes, dals, and rice. A live coal is placed in the center of a betel leaf or shallow onion peel and placed along with the other ingredients to smoke it.

Dum dena : A slow cooking process commonly called as "Dum cooking" wherein a semi-cooked ingredient is placed in a vessel and sealed with a lid covered with a flour dough. Charcoal is used for cooking.

Gil-e-hikmat: Talking of Persian influence on Awadhi cuisine, one cannot miss out on this interesting method adopted for cooking. Gilin Persian is earth or mud and hikmat implies the procedure of the hakims. When adopted for cooking purposes this method is as follows: The meat or vegetable to be cooked is generally taken whole and stuffed with nuts and spices, wrapped in a banana leaf or cloth, and covered completely with clay or multani mitti so as to seal it. Then it is buried 4-6 inches deep, and a slow fire is placed on top for 6-8 hours. The food is then dug out and is ready to be served.

Kakkori: Done on seekh. Sookha kheema used.

Moin dena: It refers to the shortening of dough. In this process fat is rubbed into the flour and made into dough for kachoris, pooris, or parathas. This makes the final product crisp, flaky, and crumbly E.g.: Warqui, parathas

Loab : This is the final stage of cooking, wherein the oil used while cooking the dish rises on top and gets separated.

Ittr : Using perfume in many dishes is the key factor in Awadhi cuisine, mainly they use perfume taken from the musk deer.

Kalai: Tin lining given to copper utensils to avert toxicity.

Dastarkhwan: Dining area.

Diwan -e-khar - Assembly/dining room for nobles

Diwan-e- am - Assembly of subjects

Lohe ka Tandoor: Made of copper with kalai . Used traditionally for making sheermal roti..

Famous Food

Kebabs: Awadh was really known for its meat dishes, especially the tender kebabs. Lucknow boasts of some of the best kebabs in India. The best way to eat a kebab is with Indian breads such as roti, chapati and naan. However, if you are in Lucknow, you can try it with ultra thin rumali rotis. These work wonders with the boti or the galawati kebabs.

Galawati Kebabs: Any discussion about the kebabs of Lucknow inevitably starts with the galawati (or galouti) kebab, considered one of the signature dishes of the city of nawabs. These special melt-in-the-mouth kebabs were originally created during the 19th century for Nawab Wajid Ali Shah who, it is rumoured, had lost his teeth but still desired the taste of kebabs. A one-armed cook named Haji Murad Ali perfected the recipe of the galawati. His son opened Tunday Kababi (or the one-armed man's kebab), a 100-year-old establishment that still serves the galawati made according to the original, secret recipe. The kebab is a circular patty made out of finely minced goat meat. Green papayas are used as a tenderiser and binding agent. Multiple spices are added to the kebab, some of which have never been divulged to the public. The patties are then roasted in ghee till brown.

Kakori Kebabs: Another famous Lucknowi creation is the kakori kebab. According to a popular story, at a party thrown by an Awadhi aristocrat, a British official made a disparaging remark about the coarse texture of the seekh kebabs. Angered by this slight, the aristocrat tasked his staff to rework on the texture of seekh kebabs. And that's the kakori kebab was born. What sets it apart? Mangoes are used to soften the meat.

Shami and Boti Kebabs: Shami kebabs are spicy round patties that are tenderised with raw green mango in the summer and karonda, a sour and acidic fruit in other seasons. Boti kebabs are small pieces of skewered lamb that are marinated in a mix of yogurt and spices and then cooked in a tandoor.

Biryani: If there's anything as famous as Lucknow's kebabs, it is its biryani. Interestingly, biryani comes from the Persian word 'birian' which means 'roasted before cooking'. The biryani of Lucknow is different as in the rice and meat is cooked separately. They are then layered and baked dum-style in a sealed handi (pot). The biryani is aromatic and has subtle flavours.

Nihari Kulcha: Non-vegetarian lovers can't leave Lucknow without trying this absolutely fantastic and lip-smacking combination. The nihari is a rich but mildly flavoured mutton gravy, and kulchas are a thick leavened bread. Together they make a better love story than Romeo and Juliet.

Sheermal: Bored with the regular rotis?Try Lucknow's sheermal. Traditionally kneaded with milk, it is a sweetened naan rich in saffron. Baked in an iron tandoor, what lends it a special taste is the sprinkling of saffron and cardamom-flavoured milk on the walls of the tandoor. Sheermal tastes great with kebabs, kormas, and even by itself. The baqarkhani is an elaborate variation of the sheermaal that is fried on a griddle instead of being baked in a tandoor. Other kinds of sheermal varieties include zafrani, and hazri sheermal. Lucknow has an entire lane dedicated to sheermals.

Awadhi Murgh Qorma: An inherent part of every royal gathering, Awadhi Murgh Qorma is engrained in the system of all Nawabs. Silky and melting in the mouth, the meat is braised in spiced sauces, butter, ground nuts and cream. The rich and velvety flavours take the seeker on a stairway to food heaven!

Murgh Massalam: This finger-licking dish was first mentioned in Abul Fazl's Ain-i-Akbari, where the royal dishes cooked in Emperor Akbar's reign were documented. It, then, went by the name Musamman. In a previous instance, it was also mentioned by 14th century traveller and scholar Ibn Battuta who described it as one of the dishes at Sultan Muhammad bin Tughlaq's court. The whole chicken is marinated in ginger-garlic paste, sometimes mixed with eggs, and seasoned with various spices to make this delicious cuisine.

Seekh Kebab: Skewered cylindrical kebabs made with minced lamb or mutton, mixed with aromatic spices and grilled to perfection. Seekh kebabs when paired with a rumali roti, raw onion rings and a mint-coriander chutney are exceptional. Squeeze a lemon wedge on these kebabs for that extra kick. These kebabs are commonly made with minced chicken meat if you are not a fan of mutton.

Mutton Do Pyaaza: A mutton curry that is so fragrant, the neighbours will come asking 'Khaane me kya banaya hai aaj?' (What's cooking?). Mutton do pyaaza is a beautifully aromatic curry made with crunchy onions, whole spices and a big dollop of ghee. Mutton do pyaaza tastes great with some boiled rice, naan or warm home made soft chapatis.

Korma – Murgh Awadhi Korma / Mutton Korma: Kormas are generally dishes made with meat and vegetables braised in a meat/vegetable stock and yogurt or cream. Kormas can be made with chicken or mutton depending on your taste and preference. Awadhi kormas are spiced with khada masalas like cinnamon, bay leaves and cardamom. These whole spices give the Awadhi curries and kormas the rich flavor we expect. A few recipes to cooke Awadhi chicken and mutton korma at home also add coconut cream to increase the depth and richness of the korma. Kormas are best enjoyed with some flaky warqi parantha.

Pasanday: The royal nawabs took their curries and kormas very seriously and their chefs made sure to leave no stone unturned to develop the most fragrant and tender meat recipes. Pasanday or pasandas are boneless mutton fillets flattened with a mallet, marinated with spices, yogurt and raw papaya. They are preferably kept marinated overnight and cooked in a pan with a generous amount of clarified butter. The marination is also added to the pan while cooking to form the gravy. These pasandas make for a hearty curry that taste great with some naan or home made rotis.

Nimona: Nimona or hare matar ka nimona is a popular vegetarian dish from the Awadh region. Fresh green peas coarsely ground and cooked in a tomato gravy with some pan fried potatoes is a delicious vegetarian recipe. A simple home style nimona with ghee smeared rotis or jeera rice tastes wonderful.

Paneer-Do-Pyaaza |Awadhi Paneer: Like mutton do pyaaza, paneer do pyaaza is cooked in lots of onions, whole spices and clarified butter. If you are not a fan of paneer, cooking this recipe with mushrooms or soya brings out equally satisfying results. Awadhi paneer is an easy recipe if you want a rich tasting vegetarian curry for your spread.

Navrattan Korma: A melange of vegetables like carrots, peas, beans, cauliflower cooked with heavy cream, nuts and fruits. Some recipes add pineapple, while some refrain from doing so. A navrattan korma is the perfect vegetarian dish if you want to enjoy some rich, thick vegetarian gravy from Awadhi cuisine. A hearty curry paired with some navrattan korma and crisp rotis.

Ulte Tawa Ka Parantha: The breads the nawabs ate were as rich as their kebabs and curries. Ulta tawa literally translates into an inverted griddle. Thin rotis cooked on the back or convex side of the tawa are a perfect accompaniment to the rich Awadhi curries and kormas. Ulta tawa paranthas can be a little sweet to taste.

Warqi Parantha: A flaky warqi roti (Varki parantha) is so delicious and rich that it can be eaten without any kormas. These yummy rotis can be made with whole wheat flour too if you do not want to use refined flour. Doused in ghee, warqi rotis taste great with Lucknowi kebabs, curries and kormas.

Malai Paan: Almost every speciality of Lucknow has a story behind it and so does Malai Paan or Bilai ki Gilori. According to local lore, it is believed that this sweet dish emerged as a result of a ban on paan by the nawabs of Lucknow. The chefs of the royal kitchen came up with Malai Paan, which looks like a paan but is prepared from milk and malai (clotted cream). Making the sweet dish is quite a task. The malai needs to be set into paper thin sheets and rolled into the shape of a paan after being filled with dry fruits and mishri (crystal sugar).

Shahi Tukda: And we finally arrive at the sweet junction, because, what is Lucknow without its mashoor mithas!? While abundant sweet dishes are famous in the city, nothing compares to the historical and authentic Shahi Tukda! Bread pieces dipped in sugar syrup sprinkled with saffron, and blended with delicious rabdi, result in this paradisal Mughlai dessert!

Kulfi: While you can get the Malai Paan packed for home too, sadly ice-creams have to be consumed on the spot. When it comes to our desi kulfis, Lucknow for sure knows how to give a royal treat to the palate of its visitors.

Makhan Malai / Nimish: A gentle tasting and extremely delicate Awadhi dessert which has been popularised in modern India as daulat ki chaat. Makhan Malai or Nimish is a dessert made with milk cream which is available only during the winter season. It is so light and airy that you could eat up an entire katori and not feel heavy after it. The main technique for the perfect makhan malai is to expose the milk to the early morning dew and churn it till it's light and airy. Sugar and cardamom powder are added for that mildly pleasant flavor.

Badaam Halwa: A Halwa so rich that it gave the royals a run for their money. Almonds soaked, ground and cooked with copious amounts of ghee. Garnished with saffron and slivered almonds, a beautifully yellow badam halwa is heavenly. Awadhi cuisine also boasts off a large variety of halwas like kaali gajar ka halwa (black carrot halwa) and kaju halwa (cashew nut halwa).

CHAPTER NINETEEN

Thai Food Festival

In Thailand, food forms a central part of any social occasion, and it often becomes the social occasion in itself or a reason to celebrate. This is partly due to the friendly, social nature of Thai people, but also because of the way in which food is ordered, served, and eaten. Family and friends unite and share through food.

The Key Flavors: A typical Thai meal includes five main flavors: salty, sweet, sour, bitter, and spicy. Indeed, most Thai dishes are not considered satisfying unless they combine all five. While the seasoning can be spicy for a foreign palate, Thai food ensures that a balance of all flavors is present.

When eating out, or making a meal at home, a group of Thai diners would eat a variety of meat and/or fish dishes, plus vegetables, a noodle dish, and possibly soup. Everything is shared, except the soup each person might order, or each person gets a personal bowl to get a serving of the soup. Dessert may consist simply of fresh fruit, such as pineapple or any of the thousands of tropical fruits that are common in the country (guava, durian, mangosteen, papayas, bananas, tamarind, or mangoes, amongst many). Or it could be something more elaborate, like colorful rice cakes, rice dumplings coated in coconut, grass jelly, or a bean dessert. Thais eat slowly and enjoy the food, as a meal is also an opportunity for sharing with loved ones.

Influences in Thai Cuisine

The flavors found in modern-day Thailand come from ancient history. As early as the 13th century, the Thai people had established what might be considered the heart of Siamese cuisine as we know it today: various types of meat and seafood combined with rice, local vegetables, herbs, and pungent garlic and pepper. Later on, the Chinese brought noodles to Thailand, as well as the most important Thai cooking tool: the steel wok. Thai cuisine is also heavily influenced by Indian spices and flavors, which is evident in its famous green, red, and yellow curries. Impossible to confuse with Indian curries, Thai curries incorporate many Indian spices in their pastes, maintaining their own unique flavors thanks to local ingredients, such as Thai holy basil, lemongrass, and galangal.

Other influences on Thai cooking come from neighboring countries, like Vietnam, Cambodia, Indonesia, Laos, Burma, and Malaysia. Such plentiful and vast influences combine to create the complex taste of present-day Thai cooking—one of the fastest-growing and most popular of world cuisines today.

Rice: Nothing occupies a more prominent place in Thai cuisine than rice. The most served dish in all meals, rice is treated with respect and never wasted. Thailand grows and serves many varieties of rice, and Jasmine is the most favored, but also the most expensive. Glutinous, or sticky rice is also fairly common, and white rice is abundant and less expensive than Jasmine rice while still being delicious. Cooks pay a lot of attention to the quality of the rice they buy and have many techniques for how to cook it, which temperature to use, how much water, how to steam it, and for how long. Rice can make or break a meal. Noodles are very common, but not as common as rice. Whereas rice is served to share, noodles dishes are often for individual consumption.

Presentation Is Important: The formal presentation of food is another important aspect of Thai culture. Attention to detail and how pretty it looks when served are relevant to the eating experience. Regardless of the beautiful flavors it provides, the dish has to look appealing, and this aspect honors the respect Thai culture has for its food and ingredients. Thai food presentation is among the most exquisite in the world; serving platters are decorated with all variety of flower-carved vegetables and fruits, palace-style stir-fries include elegantly carved vegetables within the dish itself. Chefs are trained in the art of carving because food needs an extra layer of attention beyond cooking and into the realm of the aesthetic.

Most dishes come in bite sizes, a clever way to get around the fact that Buddhism discourages cooking a whole animal. So fish, beef, pork, and chicken are sliced before cooking, alongside all of the other ingredients, also chopped and cubed.

Thai Ingredients

To cultivate a better understanding of Thai cuisine, start with these pantry staples, all of which you can find online or in Asian grocery stores:

1. Chilies: Chilies (phrik) are integral to Thai cuisine, providing a lightning strike of clarity through the muggy, tropical South Asian heat. Chilies are used as condiments, seasoning, and as a component to even the most basic of curry pastes. Fiery bird's eye chilies (phrik khi nu) come in both green and red varieties. Dried red chilies come in long, skinny forms (phrik chi fa) and as tiny, heat-packing sizes that fit in your palm (phrik haeng). You can substitute most in a pinch—green serrano peppers will work if you can't find bird's eye chilies, for example—but tracking down the real thing will prove how much multifaceted value each variety brings to the table.

2. Fish paste: An appreciation for the elusive "fifth taste," umami, is alive and well in Thai cuisine. The best way to build it is with fermented products. For delivering that unbeatable undercurrent of umami, nothing beats a few dashes of fish sauce (nam pla). Made from salted and fermented fish—strong-flavored fish like anchovies or mackerel that has been aged for up to two years—the high-quality fish sauce is simultaneously salty, sweet, and savory. Use it in marinades, dipping sauces, or dressings, or serve it as a condiment with chopped chilies alongside noodles or rice dishes.

3. Shrimp paste: Pungent, salted shrimp paste (kapi) is a powerhouse of flavor and acts as a building block for curry pastes or seasoning in dishes like fried rice.

4. Dried shrimp: Tiny, dime-sized dried shrimp (kung haeng) are mixed into curry paste or ground in a mortar and pestle for green papaya salad. Equal parts crunchy and chewy, dried shrimp are also an integral seasoning in Chinese, Korean, Burmese, and Vietnamese cooking.

5. Oyster sauce: Oyster sauce (nam man hoi), a thick, sweet, and salty sauce made from caramelized oyster liquor, is most commonly found in the cuisine of central Thailand, where Chinese influences are most prevalent. Use it to lend a boost of brine when glazing stir-fried meats and vegetables like broccoli or eggplant.

6. Coconut: Coconut is among the first ingredients that come to mind when people think of Thai food. The mellow fruit provides a lush texture to curries and soups, and its fatty, dairy-esque cooling properties restore balance to even the spiciest of dishes. The use of coconut is less common in Northerneastern Thailand's cuisine. For example, in Isan, the fresh, lighter cooking style is best exemplified by its green papaya salads (yam) and barbecue.

7. Spices and spice blends: While chilies deliver heat, spices round out how we experience that heat. Whole coriander seeds, white peppercorns, ground turmeric, black cardamom, cumin, fennel seed, and curry powder all play a role in building the seamless tour de force of any Thai dish. Spices lose their pungency the longer they sit, so stock the freshest jars you can, and avoid buying in bulk unless you have plans to use all of the spices.

8. Soy sauce: Thai cooking utilizes three different soy sauces—light, sweet, and dark. Light soy sauce, also known as thin soy sauce, is the most commonly used soy sauce in Thai cooking. Thai soy sauce is used as a dipping sauce for dishes like khao man gai, poached chicken with rice. Sweet soy sauce is a major component in stir-fries and noodle dishes, while dark soy sauce imparts color and a light sweetness into dishes like pad see ew.

9. Tamarind: Tamarind juice (or its thick, sticky paste) is a secret weapon when it comes to seasoning: The flavor of this pod fruit—sweet, sour, and with a little bit of tangy funk—does the same work of lime and sugar, with more complexity. Use tamarind as a finishing touch on curries or soups, or incorporate it into a marinade for meat: The acidity will tenderize the meat in a similar way to citrus juice. To make your tamarind liquid, soak and strain makham piak, fresh tamarind pulp, which is sold in tightly-wrapped blocks.

10. Curry paste: Thai curries are among the best vehicles for flavor because of their strong foundation: A blend of herbs, spices, and roots like galangal, which combine to become curry paste. While many Thai cooks make their own curry pastes, jarred varieties are a good way to become familiar with their distinct flavor profiles. Green curry paste is typically a blend of green chilies and garlic for heat, shallots, and galangal for a touch of allium and gingery sweetness and bright aromatics and striking color, lemongrass, Makrut lime leaves, and Thai sweet basil. Red curry swaps the green chilies for prik haeng, dried hot red chilies, and incorporates shrimp paste and spices like coriander seeds and black peppercorn. Yellow curry gets its sunny color from turmeric and curry powder, which also lends the base blend of galangal, garlic, and chilies a subtle sweetness, tempering the heat.

11. Lemongrass: Aromatics like lemongrass are half the appeal of any dish, whether by imbuing it with flavors too subtle to fully pinpoint or rising through the air in enticing curls of steam. Lemongrass, a woody, fragrant, citrusy stalk used to flavor soups, is a perennial grass that grows in tropical

climates. The tender, white core of the stalk is desired for its distinct citrus flavor and is a common ingredient in Thai, Indian, Indonesian, and Vietnamese cooking. Its lemony flavor stands up to prolonged cooking, making it perfect for slow-cooked stews and curries.

12. Galangal: Also known as "lesser ginger," galangal (kha) is the milder cousin of the spicy rhizome. Galangal, which also has a papery skin that must be peeled away before using, brings a peppery, citrus-like zing to soups like tom kha and stir-fries.

13. Turmeric root: Just like knobs of fresh ginger root, it features a thin inedible skin that's easily peeled away to reveal an electric orange flesh with the consistency of fine, wet bark. Cooking with fresh turmeric extracts more of its lively, peppery essence.

14. Makrut lime leaves: Makrut lime leaves are a step down from lemongrass, intensely fragrant in a restrained way, perfect for adding a hint of lime flavor to soups.

15. Palm sugar: Thai food often relies on the relationships between sugar, acid, and heat. Palm sugar, made from the sap of coconut palms, is typical of southern Thai dishes, while northern regions rely more on brown sugar made from sugarcane. (Neither results in an overpowering sweetness like white sugar, but instead lends a smoky, butterscotch character to desserts and sauces.)

16. Sticky rice: Like most Asian cuisines, rice (khao) is a staple component of any meal. Sticky rice, also known as glutinous rice or sweet rice, is the preferred side-dish rice in Northern and Northeastern Thailand and Laos, where cooked rice is used as a vehicle for all kinds of savory dishes and desserts like khao niaow ma muang, mango sticky rice served with coconut custard and fresh mango. Sticky rice varieties from Laos and Northern Thailand tend to have a longer grain and more floral scent than Japanese varieties.

17. Jasmine rice: Jasmine rice is softer, thicker, and more clingy than other kinds of aromatic rice like basmati. Jasmine rice is the perfect side dish for all types of Thai foods, including grilled or ground meats and spicy curries. The stickiness and sweetness of jasmine rice make it a great addition to stir-fried vegetables and stands up well to a stew. (Due to its soft texture, it may not be the best choice for fried rice.)

18. Noodles: Dried rice noodles are a crucial ingredient in any Thai pantry: Keep wide, flat rice noodle varieties for substantial stir-fries, and thinner rice noodles for dishes like pad thai, soups, or chilled salads with

peanut sauce. Thai cuisine also features egg noodles, cellophane noodles, and bean thread noodles.

19. Cilantro: Herbs are not just for garnishes in Thai cuisine—they provide a fresh note to the complex symphony taking place in every dish. Cilantro, whether finely minced into a curry paste, or served atop curries, noodles, or stir-fries, lends a cooling, grassy brightness. If you can find it, cilantro root can also be used to add the herb's signature floral essence to soups and stews.

20. Thai basil: This type of basil, which comes with both green and purple leaves, is more pungent than the Genovese basil used to top pizzas, with a sweetness tinged with earthy, savory bite. A variety called "holy basil" is also frequently used, which has more noticeable licorice or anise flavor. Learn more about Thai basil.

Thai Food Dishes

Snacks Galore: Aside from meals, Thais are renowned "snackers". It is easy to pick up a quick but delicious snack for mere pennies along the roadside or at marketplaces in Thailand. Popular snacks consist of spring rolls, chicken or beef satay, raw vegetables with spicy dip, soups, salads, and sweets.

Pad Kra Pao Moo (Minced Pork Stir-Fried with Chilli and Thai Basil): Forget Pad Thai. Straight into the top spot is Pad Kra Pao Moo. This dish consists of stirfried minced pork with lots of chilies, garlic, onion, green beans, and Thai basil served over rice. This is a classic dish eaten almost daily by many Thai locals, and is extremely popular with travelers also. A serious contender in the most-loved Thai food category, this dish is delicious, spicy, and found in every restaurant, and at most street food vendors. Tip: ADD a fried egg to balance out the spice.

Tom Kha Gai (Coconut Soup with Chicken): Tom Kha Gai is a soup rich in coconut milk and galangal root, made with earthy Asian mushrooms and tender chicken. It contains fragrant ingredients, such as lemongrass and kaffir lime leaves, giving it a slightly sour taste. Sprigs of cilantro add a delicious freshness. Chilli is optional in this dish, so Tom Kha Gai is an excellent choice for those that aren't so keen on lots of spice.

Khao Pad (Fried Rice): However, Thai fried rice can be cooked with chicken, beef, pork, or vegetables. Either option is delicious. Fried rice is made with various ingredients, and no two servings will ever be the same. Thai cooks use whatever is on hand, which commonly includes garlic, onion, egg, meat, and fish sauce. Tip: Try adding a squeeze of lime and sprinkle of chili flakes.

Pad Thai (Thai Fried Noodles): A dish that has become synonymous with Thai cuisine, Pad Thai is a well-loved stir-fried noodle dish served in every kind of establishment imaginable, from street stalls all the way up to Michelin star restaurants. Loved for its peanutty flavor, you'll also find tofu cubes, egg, and crunchy bean sprouts sprinkled throughout or piled next to the noodles. Choose your favorite protein, add a squeeze of lime and let your taste buds dance.

Moo Satay (Pork Satay): This classic Asian snack can be found widely throughout South-East Asia and is loved by Thais and foreigners alike. Traditionally satay is barbequed meat marinated in turmeric and coconut milk, put on a skewer served with a rich and indulgent peanut sauce. Commonly pork or chicken is used. However, you will find that the choice of meat may vary from restaurant to restaurant. Perfect as a starter or an afternoon snack.

Tom Yum Goong (Sweet and Sour Soup with Prawns): Tom Kha Gai's not-so-distant, spicier and fishier cousin, Tom Yum, is a clear soup with the perfect balance of sweet and sour flavors. You'll find mushrooms, tomatoes, lemongrass, lime juice, galangal, chilies, kaffir lime leaves, onions, and fresh juicy prawns swimming throughout, with a blend of other secret herbs and spices to create this taste sensation. The exotic flavors of Tom Yum perfectly encapsulate the tastes of Thailand.

Khao Niew Mamuang (Mango with Sticky Rice): Khao Niew Mamuang may be the only dessert to get a mention, but our list would not be complete without it. This simple, traditional Thai dessert is made by pairing fresh mango with sweetened sticky rice served with coconut milk. Well-loved by locals, it is available all year round but is cheapest and freshest during Thailand's mango season, from April to May.

Kai Yad Sai (Stuffed Thai Omelet): Made famous by Jay Fai and her Michelin-star Bangkok street-food restaurant, this stuffed omelet is becoming increasingly popular in Thai cuisine. Traditionally, a beaten egg is stuffed with minced pork and vegetables with a tangy sauce but there are plenty of other possible fillings. Jay Fai has pushed the boundaries and created her own version of the dish. Her seafood-heavy menu includes a thin egg omelet filled with succulent chunks of sweet crab.

Khao Soi (Curried Noodle Soup): This dish from Northern Thailand, with influences from Laos and Myanmar, is slowly making its way down south due as its popularity spreads. Created with a mix of boiled and crispy egg noodles, Khao Soi is a curry-flavored thick coconut broth with pickled mustard greens, shallots, lime, and ground chilies fried in oil, and served with succulent chicken on the bone.

Pad See Ew (Fried Flat Noodle with Soy Sauce): Another yummy and frequently ordered Thai noodle dish is Pad See Ew. Large, flat rice noodles are cooked with lashings of garlic, onion, egg, cabbage, and your choice of protein. Soy sauce is mixed through to give the dish its well-known dark color. Eat like a local, add a sprinkle of chili flakes and chili vinegar, and enjoy.

Laab Moo (Minced Pork Salad): Laab is originally a Northeastern (Isaan) dish, but is enjoyed throughout Thailand. It is usually served as part of a set meal with papaya salad and rice. Minced pork is combined with lime juice, fish sauce, chili flakes, fresh herbs, and toasted rice for crunch. Though minced pork is the common ingredient, Laab is also often made with chicken or duck.

Gaeng Panang (Panang Curry): Panang is made using a thick curry paste with cilantro seeds, cumin seeds, red curry paste, shrimp sauce, and peanuts. The paste is then combined with coconut milk to create its well-known creamy flavor. Add some kaffir lime leaves for a fresh taste, and slow cook your onion, potato, and meat in the sauce until tender and delicious. Serve with rice for a rich, indulgent, hearty meal. Heaven.

Gai Pad Med Ma Muang (Stir-Fried Chicken with Cashew Nuts): Chicken pieces and cashew nuts are deep-fried to become the bulk of this mouthwatering dish. Onions, garlic, shallots, chillis, and often brightly colored bell peppers are then combined with the holy grail of Thai cooking sauces: soy, oyster, and fish, to finish off. Easy to find and even easier to fall in love with.

Som Tam (Spicy Green Papaya Salad): Salads aren't often found in Thailand, and this Thai salad won't fit your view of a conventional Western salad. Som Tam is incredibly simple, but packs a punch and is full of flavor. This dish is made by pounding a variety of ingredients together in a pestle and mortar. Som Tam includes garlic, chilies, fish sauce, peanuts, dried shrimp, tomatoes, sugar, lime juice, green beans, peanuts, and of course, grated sour green papaya.

There are a few variations to the traditional Som Tam that are also worth a try.

Som Tam Thai – Green papaya salad dressed with fish sauce and lime juice.

Som Tam Boo – With fermented crab.

Som Tam Pla Raa – With fermented fish.

Som Tam Hoy Dong – With fermented oysters.

Fresh, simple, and delicious.

Poh Pia Tod (Thai Spring Rolls): Everyone loves a spring roll, but Thai folk really do know how to make them well. Perfect as an appetizer or to grab from a street vendor after a few Chang beers, Thai spring rolls hit the spot every single time. Carrot, cabbage, mushroom, and onion are mixed with rice noodles before being rolled into their spring roll wrapper and fried until perfectly crispy and golden. Choose your meat – they have them all – or leave it without. It is entirely up to you!

Tip: Dip into sweet chili or plum sauce for an addictive treat.

Gaeng Massaman (Massaman Curry): Massaman curry is similar to Penang curry in its look and textures. It is mild, sweet, tangy, and peanutty, and, as with many Thai dishes, it has a coconut cream base, making it rich and delicious. It is, of course, elevated with a plethora of herbs and spices, including bay leaves, cinnamon, cumin, cilantro, galangal, lemongrass, nutmeg... the list goes on! Massaman curry is derived from Indian dishes, and has a Persian influence. There is a distinct lack of vegetables in this curry, with only onion and potato making an appearance. So, serve with some rice and embrace the double carbs!

Pla Kapung Nueng Manao (Steamed Fish with Spicy Lime Sauce): Thailand has access to some of the best and freshest fish in the world. If you walk along any busy seaside street in Thailand, you will see rows of restaurants with their catch of the day on the ice, ready to be cooked for you to enjoy. Barramundi (Asian Seabass) or Red Snapper are the locals' choice. Fresh off the boat, steamed and served with a sharp limey sauce with an abundance of raw garlic, cilantro, and chili. Fresh and flavorsome. This dish is definitely one of the healthier choices in Thailand.

Tod Mun Pla (Thai Fish Cake): Another tasty Thai appetizer is this fish cake. It is made using fresh fish, Thai basil, lime leaves, and green beans, formed into round patties before being deep-fried. Piled high on a plate, Tod Mun Pla are served with a spicy dip, usually containing cucumber, peanut, shallot, chili, vinegar, sugar and, fish sauce.

Tip: Add a side of rice or noodles to enjoy as a main meal.

Gaeng Ped (Red Curry), Gaeng Garee (Yellow Curry), Gaeng Keow Wan (Green Curry): Red, Yellow, and Green curry are undoubtedly the most famous of all the Thai curries. Each carries similar ingredients such as garlic, shallot, shrimp paste, lemongrass, and galangal. They do, however, have some crucial differences.

Red Curry uses red curry paste, which provides its vibrant color and is heavily spiced with red chili.

Yellow Curry uses turmeric and is rich in taste and color.

Green Curry is spiked with fresh green chillies, and draws on cilantro, lime leaves, and basil for its vibrant green color.

Each type is made with coconut milk for a creamy balance, and is delicious when served with rice.

Moo Ping (Barbequed Marinated Pork Skewers): A favorite for those on the go, pork shoulder is thinly sliced and marinated in cilantro root, pepper, garlic, and oyster sauce. It is lightly barbequed over charcoal and served with sticky rice. This classic snack can be found at every street vendor and night market in the country. Each vendor will have their own special marinade, so you will never taste the same Moo Ping twice. It is a breakfast favorite among locals.

Hoy Tod (Oyster Omelet): This dish will have you shamelessly licking your plate clean. Hoy Tod translates as "deep-fried oysters" but this is more like a big crispy omelet laced with juicy, fresh oysters. It is served on a bed of bean sprouts and topped with black pepper and cilantro. Simple yet heavenly.

Kuay Teow Reua (Thai Boat Noodles): Gaining its name from the vendors who sell it directly from boats, these Thai Boat Noodles are treasured. The beautifully dark, rich broth is the main event in this meal, with the secret ingredient being pig's blood. Keep an open mind, these noodles are sure to leave you wanting more.

Mu Kratha (Thai Barbeque): Influenced by Korean BBQ and Chinese Hotpot, Mu Kratha is the Thai version of a tabletop barbeque, directly translating as "pan pork". It's a great choice for for a relaxing meal with friends or family, accompanied by a few drinks. There are no specific ingredients to this meal, just choose your favorite meat, fish, or vegetables and get cooking! The domed hot plate surface can be used for grilling meats, and the bottom moat contains a fragrant broth to cook your vegetables.

Khao Pad Sapparod (Pineapple Fried Rice): Always popular, Thai fried rice with shrimps and pineapple is easy to cook and very satisfying to eat. Thai jasmine rice, fresh shrimps, and pineapple are what make this dish worthy of being on this best Thai food list. Curry powder, shrimp sauce, oyster sauce, and fish sauce are the major sauces that give this dish a delicious taste.

Mah Hor (Galloping Horses): A small snack that originated inside the royal palace is something you have to try. Mah hor is delicate, but richly flavored, and it is made with mandarin orange or pineapple and topped with pork, chicken, peanuts, sugar, peppercorns, and coriander. The result is a combination of sweet fruit with a savory topping, and the taste is hard to forget.

CHAPTER TWENTY

Mexican Food Festival

Mexico has a long and rich culinary history that began long before the arrival of the Spanish. In this article we'll take a look at Mexican food culture through the ages and how it shaped the diverse, delicious cuisine we associate with Mexico today. There are three main influences on Mexican cuisine as we know it: the Mayans, the Aztecs, and the Spanish. Before we dive into the cuisine though, let's take a brief look at the timeline of pre-Mexican and Mexican history.

THE MAYAN INFLUENCE: The Mayans were a largely nomadic civilization whose cuisine had a great influence on the history of Mexican food culture. One staple of Mayan cuisine was corn, which was one of the few foods that was farmed on a large scale. In fact, we have the Mayans to thank for inventing the earliest form of the tortilla, a food that is central to Mexican cuisine today. The Mayans often ate tortillas with a paste made from beans given that meat was scarce in the region where they lived. Although corn and beans were staples, the Mayans were essentially hunters and gatherers, so they also caught wild game, picked tropical fruit, and fished, all of which added variety and flavor to their cuisine. Another important food in Mayan cuisine was chocolate, which was considered a gift from the Gods that had medicinal and mystical properties. (However, the Olmecs are believed to be the original makers of chocolate.) Several foods and ingredients that were invented and cultivated by the Mayans remained popular during the Aztec Empire. However, they added salt, peppers, and domesticated game such as turkey and ducks to their diet. In fact, salt and chili peppers were so essential to Aztec cuisine that it was considered fasting if one abstained from eating these two ingredients. When Hernan Cortes and the Spanish arrived in the Aztec city of Tenochtitlan in 1519, it is said he was invited to drink with King Moctezuma II,. However, it wasn't fermented grapes he was offered, but a hot cup of xocolatl, a drink made from the dark brown beans that would soon be on the European import list and as valued as the gold Hernan had come to collect.

THE SPANISH INFLUENCE: When the Spanish invaded the Aztec empire, they brought with them their own dishes, ingredients, and cooking methods. Notably, they brought new livestock such as sheep, pigs, goats, and cows which introduced a whole new array of dishes and a reliable source of protein. The introduction of livestock also led to the introduction of new dairy products, specifically cheese. which became a prominent part of the cuisine. They also brought garlic, olive oil, cinnamon, coriander, and rice, many of which are still cornerstones of Mexican cuisine. Apart from the traditional Spanish cuisine, the invasion of Mexico by the Spaniards also led to the assimilation of foods and ingredients from other Spanish colonies and trading partners. Some of these cuisines included Caribbean, French, Portuguese, and West African Cuisines. Cultural exchanges after colonial conquests never just went one way, and the invasion saw Mexico gain ingredients and cooking techniques from Europe which fueled the next stage of its culinary evolution. While the conquistadors hoped to largely do away with the local cuisine and transplant the Iberian palate to America, indegenous culinary roots ran too deep to be easily displaced. A cultural grafting took place where the assimilation of once foreign elements began to produce some of today's most recognizable Mexican dishes.

THE AMERICAN INFLUENCE: When Spain invaded Mexico, they also invaded the land that is now Texas. For the next two centuries, the Spanish colonized the region in which Native Americans were living, which led to an amalgamation of the two cultures. When Mexico gained their independence, Texas was still part of their territory. It seceded from Mexico in 1836 and became a part of the United States in 1845. Being a state meant that new foods were available in Texas such as beef, wheat, cheddar cheese, and cumin. Tejanos, the name for people of Mexican descent living in Texas, incorporated these new foods into traditional Mexican dishes. Eventually this new variation of Mexican food gained popularity and was coined TexMex cuisine. Some foods distinct to Tex-Mex cuisine are wheat tortillas, burritos, and nachos.

NORTHERN MEXICO: Interestingly, half the country is known as 'the north' with typical northern Mexican cuisine known for its cheese and meat dishes. Seafood is also common in the region along with baby goat. The most famous dishes in this part of Mexico are the burrito, cabrito, and carne asada. The north Pacific coast is popular for its fruits and vegetables. This is the area where the country gets its staple grain and fruits. The chiles and cheese that Mexico is known for are also grown and produced here. Do you love tequila? You would be elated to know that Jalisco is the area that produces this iconic drink. Head to the Bajio region for pork, sausage, and rice dishes. Apart from the pork dishes, this region is famous for desserts like cajeta, chinga, and bunuelos.

SOUTHERN MEXICO: Southern Mexican cuisine uses chili peppers of different varieties. Chicken and cheese are also famous here. If you are interested in trying indigenous Mexican fare, this is the place to head to. Regional chili peppers, mole varieties, and chocolate are used in the dishes. There are lesser known herbs such as hoja santa that are used to create unique dishes. Black beans are common in this region. Moving further south, you would find corn and spices in abundance. It's interesting to note that the cuisine of this area is different from the rest of the world. You would find Mayan influences as well as the impact of Cuban and Caribbean cuisine. Even food from Europe, Asia, and some Middle Eastern countries have a deep impact on the cuisine here. Again, corn is the basic staple of this region. Spices like achiote are used in food preparation. Conchinita pibil (slow roasted pork) is the most popular dish.

THE GULF MEXICO REGION: Finally, we reach the Gulf. Vanilla is native to this part of Mexico and hence features in many dishes along with corn. The cuisine is a blend of Mexican, Spanish, and Afro-Cuban which makes it more delectable. You would find people using herbs like thyme, parsley, marjoram, and cilantro, which were brought by the Europeans. Seafood is very common here along with dishes like chicken and peanut sauce. Anyone who has ever tried Tobasco has become its fan, and this hot sauce is named after a state here. If you happen to be in Tabasco, try the seafood here. It is mindblowing.

CENTRAL MEXICO: Central Mexico, which contains Mexico City, is the melting pot of Mexican cuisine. You will find cuisine from other parts of Mexico as well as foreign countries prevalent here. This is the place to give your palate a real gastronomical experience with taco stands and lunch stands located on every street. As a beginner, try carnitas, moles, birra, and tortas. Experiment with pre-Hispanic food if your heart desires.

STREET FOOD: High quality street food can be found all over the country, and it is often the first choice of office workers coming out for sun and sustenance in the afternoon. Selecting what to eat can be the hardest part; with a choice of slow cooked pulled pork barbacoa tacos, mushroom and soft cheese in blue corn tortillas, and chicken grilled with smoky chipotle chilies, vendors from all over Mexico have got fine dining on the fly down to an art form.

INGREDIENTS USED IN MEXICAN DISHES

Original Mexican dishes used only ingredients available locally. The cooking method was also indigenous and developed through the centuries. The basic ingredients were corn, beans, amaranth, chia, squash, avocados, limes, and tomatoes.

Saying corn is the staple of Mexico would be an understatement. It is the most common item and used to make masa, a dough that is used in many popular dishes, tortillas, and tamales.

Mexican cheese is soft and crumbly and adds a distinct taste to local dishes.

Now we can't talk about Mexican food without mentioning chillies. Mexico uses different types of chilies and they go in everything from soups to salsa. Moreover, they are used whole, fresh, smoked, dried, or powdered.

Mexican chocolate also has a distinct taste. It is bitter and of an earthy flavor that makes Mexican desserts like flan and mousse unique and delicious.

Butter is not a traditional Mexican ingredient, instead lard was used as the cooking medium. It gives the dishes a unique taste, however, nowadays people use more vegetable oil.

You may consider lime a simple item, but to a Mexican chef, it is the secret tool that adds a special zing. Be it tacos or salsa, without lime, it won't taste as good.

Chipotles, or smoke dried jalapenos, contain heat and a smoky flavor that's used in many dishes of Mexico.

Do you love the tangy flavor in Mexican fare? It usually comes from crema, sour cream that chefs use profusely.

Oregano has become a part of many international dishes, but the oregano used in Mexican dishes are more savory and aggressive....no wonder they make Mexican food so tasty and spicy.

Tomatoes are another ingredient used in Mexican cuisine to add taste and thickness to sauces.

Mexican food can also include lots of avocados (loved by everybody). It's a Mexican staple that they consume in salads, sandwiches, and (of course) guacamole.

There are also a few exotic ingredients that are used in Mexican food like the mole. This is made of more than 30 different spices. You may be surprised to know that cactus is also used in cooking.

Many of Mexico's most emblematic dishes are linked to festivals and holidays, where friends and families will gather to celebrate a saint, a wedding, a baptism, or a town anniversary. Eating and sharing meals is intrinsic to social life in Mexico.

Popular Mexican Food

Chilaquiles: Chilaquiles is definitely the most popular breakfast in the country. Made of triangular pieces of fried or toasted corn tortilla, called totopos, soaked in a red or green hot sauce, topped with shredded chicken, chorizo, shredded beef, and scrambled or sunny side up egg. It is decorated with fresh cheese, coriander, and sliced onion and is served with fried beans on the side.

Huevos Rancheros (Ranch Eggs): These represent the hats of two ranchmen. It´s made with two fried corn tortillas, topped with fried beans, and two sunny side up eggs all bathed in red hot sauce and decorated with coriander and freshly ground black pepper.

Machaca (Shredded Dried Beef): This is one of the most popular dishes on the northern side of México. Machaca is very versatile; you can either eat it in a taco, a stuffed burrito, flautas, or just as a stew with some tortillas, beans, or rice on the side. Machaca is simply a shredded version of dried beef with a proper seasoning. It´s delicious!

Discada (Plow disc BBQ): A northern meaty dish, yes... it´s full of meat: sausage, chorizo, ground meat, ham, bacon, lard, jalapeño pepper, onion. And it is all seasoned with thyme, celery, cumin, oregano, bay leaf, black pepper, black sauces, salt, rosemary, a bit of dark beer, etc. This dish is cooked on a plow disc previously cured over some wood. It is a traditional dish for family reunions.

Tacos: Recognized as the most popular Mexican dish worldwide, the taco has become an art. Some say is the "art of eating with tortilla" and, of course, Mexicans would never deny a taco to anybody. Hundreds of fillings can be put on a corn tortilla! The most common are beef steak, flank steak, chorizo, offal, "al pastor", hot and sweet marinated pork. Exotic tacos are filled with fried brains, beef´s eyes, liver with onions, scorpions, bull testicles, escamoles, and a whole lot of fillings you could never imagine. Escamoles are ant larvae found only in central and southern México. The larvae are only found once a year and harvesting them is quite a delicate operation, making this a very expensive dish—a bit like caviar.

Burritos: This is very popular on the northern side of México, especially the states bordering the United States. A burrito is a cylindrically rolled flour tortilla stuffed with different ingredients of choice, often a stew. The most popular are the fried bean burrito with cheese and the machaca burrito.

Pozole de Pollo o Guajolote (Chicken or Wild Turkey Stew): There is a myth in Mexican culture that before the conquest, Pozole was made out of human flesh. In reality, it is a dish made with the meat of a Xoloitzcuintle (a dog endemic to the country). Nowadays, though, Pozole is cooked with shredded chicken or wild turkey. There are several types, such as green, red, or white pozole, camagua, sea food, elopozole, etc. The most popular are the green and red.

Menudo (Pork Stew): History tells us this came from Spain decades before the conquest. They used pieces of tripe. Nowadays, menudo is a seasoned soup made with corn kernels, with or without the grains, and beef tripe. It is often also known as Pancita.

Cochinita Pibil (Pibil Pork Stew): A southern delight, Cochinita Pibil is a slow cooked shredded pork stew, typical of the Yucatan Peninsula. The meat is marinated in achiote, orange juice, onion, and vinegar, then cooked wrapped in banana leaves. It is served with marinated onion and fresh habanero. You can try it in tacos, burritos, tortillas... etc.

Tamales: Tamales are an icon of Mexican food. You can eat these all day every day, especially on the Day of The Candelaria. It comes from pre-Hispanic America, and is náhuatl in the indigenous language, meaning wrapped. These can be wrapped in corn leaves or banana leaves and stuffed with any stew of your choice. The most common are mole, shredded chicken or pork with green or red salsa, pepper with cheese, and yellow corn kernels.

Quesadilla: Quesadilla (Cheese-adilla) are corn or flour tortilla folded in half, stuffed with cheese or other ingredients, deep fried or grilled and eaten hot. The picture shows a blue corn quesadilla, filled with Cochinita Pibil and, of course, cheese.

Frijoles Puercos (Fried Beans): Pork beans are very popular. They are a mixture of beans cooked with lard, chorizo, bacon, cheese, serrano peppers and some other secret ingredients, making this a delicious dish.

Enchiladas: This is fast food made from corn tortilla dipped in hot sauce, filled with various stews, vegetables or proteins, depending on the style.

Enchilada is en-chili-ada—so always expect a tasty spicy touch. They are served with sour cream, fresh cheese, onion, and celery.

Chile en Nogada (Nogada Pepper): This dish comes from a very old tradition. It is made with a full Poblano pepper stuffed with picadillo (a mixture of grounded meat, fruits, and spices), topped with a walnut-based cream sauce, and decorated with pomegranate seeds and celery. From the city of Puebla, the colors resemble the Mexican flag.

Esquites (Corn Stew): Esquites are a delicious street food and come in many different varieties depending on where you are in the country. Northern states put cream, mayonnaise, chili powder, lemon, butter, and cheese on it. Here, you can either eat it in a cup or with the whole corn pierced on a stick. The central-southern states prefer them with cream and cheese or with lemon chili powder, but not a mix. Some people cook them with epazote and bone marrow. Extremely delicious!

Alegria de Amaranto (Amaranth Hard Joy Candy): Mexican popped amaranth hard candy comes as a bar with various toppings, for example, dried fruit, chocolate, raisins, nuts, etc. This candy is made from amaranth seeds mixed with honey. It is originally from México City, and, since the 16th century, it has been known by the name Alegría, which means joy.

Mole: Mole is a sauce made from a mixture of dried chilies, tomatoes, chocolate, seeds, and spices. It is one of México´s most representative dishes. There are several versions of its origin. One of them says that Poblano Mole, whose original recipe involved about 100 ingredients, emerged in the Convent of Santa Rosa in the city of Puebla, when a nun ground in a metate different chilies and seasonings. Another version says that Archbishop Juan de Palafox from Spain came to visit Puebla. One of the cooks got so nervous that he stumbled into the casserole where guajolotes (wild turkeys) were cooking and chilies, almonds, chocolate, and other spices fell in. In México, there are seven different types of mole; you should try each one.

Pipián: Pipián stew originated in pre-Hispanic times and was one of Emperor Moctezuma´s favorite foods. Coming from the central-southern states, it is obligatory on any sauce menu. The sauce is made from toasted and ground pumpkin seeds and usually poultry, although it is sometimes accompanied by pork, beef, or rabbit.

Aguachile (Chili Water): This is a typical dish of the western coast region of México, particularly the state of Sinaloa. It is said that pre-Hispanic cultures used to mix dry meat with water and chilies (chiltepín chili). In 1970, they replaced meat with raw shrimp and added other ingredients: lime juice, cucumber, coriander, red onion, avocado, salt, and pepper.

Ceviche: Originating in Peru, ceviche is part of South and Central American gastronomic culture. The basics always include raw fish, onion, tomato, chilies, coriander, and lemon. The most commonly used proteins are fish, shrimp, clam, octopus, crab, or snail.

Pescado Zarandeado (Stirred Fish): This is a very popular dish from the Mexican coasts and it's a pre-Hispanic delight. Zarandear is a term that means moving or shaking a lot. The meat was originally roasted on a mangrove wood grill called Zaranda, but now a metal grill is used. It is prepared by seasoning the fish with lemon and chili sauce, then smoking it with mangrove wood.

Camarones a la Diabla (Deviled Shrimp): One of the most ingrained traditions in Mexico is Lent, when seafood is usually eaten instead of meat. Camarones a la Diabla is an iconic dish during the season. It is cooked with a combination of chilies—guajillo, chipotle and arbol—which makes it extremely spicy.

Birria de Chivo (Goat Stew): From the State of Jalisco, this dish is seasoned with a preparation based on some varieties of chili, seasonings, and salt. A tomato-based sauce is prepared with the juices from the cooking, called consomé. Birria was originally made with goat, but lamb, mutton, pork, chicken, veal, beef, or fish can also be used. Some birrias are cooked over the heat in covered pots, with the lid sometimes sealed with corn dough. Baked birrias are called tatemadas. Originally, the meat was wrapped in maguey pencas and cooked, but this tradition has almost disappeared.

Tlayuda: This is the most famous dish in the State of Oaxaca, southern México. It is a large corn tortilla (about 30 cm in diameter) made of white corn. It is first put on the griddle and then placed on the embers to get it dry and crispy. A traditional tlayuda consists of lard, black beans, tasajo (dried pork meat), chorizo, and cheese and is accompanied by water chili, sliced tomato, avocado, and, of course, you can´t leave out the mezcal with worm salt!

Guacamole con Chapulines (Guacamole with Grasshoppers): You can find this in the state of Oaxaca and México City. It is the perfect combination of creamy avocado and crispy, acidic grasshopper. They are delicious and very nutritious as they have a high protein content. Marinated with salt and garlic, then sautéed on the griddle until they turn reddish and crispy, they are a surprising treat.

Flautas (Flutes): The flutes are traditional Mexican tacos made with rolled corn tortilla and filled with mashed potato, cheese, chicken, etc. The difference is that they´re fried in oil. They´re usually served with coriander, tomato, fresh cheese, and sour cream on top.

Torta Ahogada (Drowned Baguette): This is the most popular street food in the state of Jalisco. It's a sandwich made with a bread called birote stuffed with confit pork meat immersed in a hot sauce based on dried chilies, vinegar, tomato, and spices. They are simple, spicy and tasty! The original torta ahogada is eaten out of a plastic bag.

Carnitas (Confit Pork Meat): This is different parts of pork fried in lard, cooked in huge copper pots for hours. The secret tasty flavor comes from the various ingredients used in the cooking process, one of them being orange juice or soda! You can eat it in a taco or a sandwich.

Caldo Azteca (Aztec Soup): Here´s a great classic of Mexican cuisine, made with strips of fried tortillas topped with chicken broth, tomato, pepper, garlic, and onion, scented with epazote and coriander, and topped with cheese, avocado, and sour cream. In Tlaxcala city, Aztec soup was born as a hybrid, combining Mexican corn tortilla with the Spanish tradition of soup making.

Gorditas de Nata (Mini Cream Pancakes): This is a fluffy dessert served outside churches as an after-mass treat, especially on Sundays. They are made from wheat flour, cream, sugar, and cinnamon and can be eaten plain or filled.

CHAPTER TWENTY-ONE

Lost Recipe Feast

As we move further with time, cuisine changes with every decade, where some recipes are modified, and some get lost with time. Also, recipes that actually are an amalgamation of various cuisines are attracting foodies. There are lots of mouth-watering local dishes that haven't been a part of our diet for a long time. There are several recipes that have slipped from our kitchen. With time, we are drawn more towards calorie-based diets and ready-to-eat meals.

Chitt : This gravy made up of ginger-garlic was a common dish that was cooked in many Punjabi households. Known for its immunity-boosting benefits, this dish was also considered a perfect remedy for sore throat. This dish has milk or curd which gives it a creamier texture.

Shikar Da Aachar :India has a special love for pickles. This non-vegetarian pickle is made up of quail meat, vinegar, mustard oil, and so many other spices. This pickle has lost its significance these days but needs to be revived. Using vinegar is quite essential in this pickle as it helps in increasing the pickle's shelf life.

Ganne Wale Chawal: Also known as raawh wale chaawal in Punjab and rasawal in old Lucknow, this is actually a slow-cooked dish in which rice is cooked on low flame with sugarcane juice and later garnished with nuts. Earlier it was cooked in Lohri celebrations but now has lost its significance.

Phulkari Pulao : This rich dish is connected to the regime of Maharaja Ranjit Singh in Patiala. Made with curd and khoya, this dish has beautiful spots and thus, resembles Phulkari. When garnished with dry fruits and pomegranate seeds, this dish can show you a really good time.

Mutton Taka Tak : There are so many mutton dishes from Punjab that we absolutely love. This is one such mutton delicacy that is absolutely delicious and thus needs the limelight. These crispy mutton cutlets with sprinkled garam masala and whole coriander were commonly sold as street food in Punjab but now have got lost.

Paani ki Roti: This roti is from the rural areas of Uttar Pradesh and Haryana. Frequently made in our ancestral village, Saag (a dish made from leafy vegetables) is served with it. The dough is made using wet hands, and further, a layer of water on the sides of the roti gives it a unique flavor. Despite being cooked on a griddle, it tastes like Chulhe ki roti.

Sannata: Quite a weird name, right? But there's a history behind it. The ingredients being caraway seeds, mint, asafoetida, rock salt, black salt, and buttermilk, it provides relief in irritable bowel movements and makes peace, or say, it silences all the stomach issues (Sannata means Silence in Hindi). It is often confused with raita, but the consistency differs. A glass of sannata contains one part curd and three parts of water.

Dadpe Pohe: A relatively unpopular sibling of the traditional poha (flattened rice cooked with onions and spices), it is a coconut-infused flattened rice snack and belongs to the Maharashtra region.

Khus Sharbat: A summer cooling drink made from a fragrant and cooling herb called khus or vetiver.

Dal Fara: They are mustard and curry leave tempered, and lentils (chana dal and urad dal) stuffed dumplings. They have originated from Eastern Uttar Pradesh and are served with coriander or mint chutney.

Gobhi Danthal: It is cauliflower stems in spicy and tangy gravy; Tandoori Rotis are served with it. It originally belongs to Punjab.

Kapoorkand: It is made only two ingredients i.e. bottle gourd and sugar. Kapoorkand are sugar-coated threads of the much-underestimated vegetable – bottle gourd, that can be stored up to a fortnight. It is something that melts into mouth.

Paani ki Gujiya: Unlike the usual gujiya, they are made with rice flour and are steamed and not fried. It belongs to the Braj region of Uttar Pradesh and Chambal in Madhya Pradesh.

Rasaawar: It is somewhat similar to kheer. But, unlike kheer, the amount of milk used is negligible. Ideally, for a liter of sugarcane juice, only 30 ml of milk is needed. Adding dry-fruits would overshadow the aroma of sugarcane. Thus, for authentic preparation, rasaawar is made without dry-fruits.

Meenja: These are small balls made of besan (gram flour) with salt, oil, and red chili powder in it, mixed in spicy onion gravy. The dish basically belongs to Rajasthan.

Dahi ki Arbi: These are taro roots in spicy yogurt gravy. Like every traditional dish, it requires us to stand in the kitchen for long hours continuously stirring, so that it doesn't split.

Badal Jam: Badal Jam is an Awadhi appetizer of shallow fried brinjal, spicy onion, tomato, and tangy garlic-flavored yogurt sauce with a mixture of mint or coriander leaves.

Karara: Moong dal is made into a paste and mixed with buttermilk and spices. It is stirred until it gets a thick consistency.

Hing Aam Achaar: Not even a single drop of oil is used to make this achar. The essence of asafoetida being the significant character, the taste is way different from that of usual mango pickle.

Shufta Kanaguchhi: Soaked dry fruits fried with cottage cheese and cooked with sugar syrup and spices; it is a dessert from Jammu & Kashmir, especially made during weddings.

Tootak: A Hyderabadi starter, tootak are semolina and condensed milk dumplings, stuffed with cottage cheese, potatoes, and dry fruits, fried together in spices with a dash of lemon.

Tawsali: A traditional Goan recipe, it is made from cucumbers, more preferably the yellow ones. Apart from cucumbers, jaggery, semolina, and coconut are also added. Though it's a cake it is steamed, and not baked.

Tirre ki Roti: The flour is a combination of wheat, barley and gram flour. With every morsel, one feels that the aroma of one grain is trying to dominate that of the other grain, making it tastier with every bite. It is served hot from the griddle and is deeply soaked in clarified butter.

Malai ka Paan: Originated during the times of the nawabs, it is a paan without betel leaf and made of milk and malai instead! It requires tedious work for malai to be made into paper-thin sheets and rolled like a paan. It is filled with mishri and dry fruits.

Boote ka Samosa: These are samosas stuffed with green grams instead of potatoes.

Parinde mein parinda (Uttar Pradesh) : The dish's pre-preparation takes a lot of effort. It takes a lot of patience to make this since the flavours need to be expertly sealed inside. It is a recreation of the bigger roast, which was essentially created from the entire camel, which was then packed with much smaller animals, one within the other, until the smallest hollow was filled with a cooked egg. A boiled egg, duck, chicken, and quail were used in its preparation. Each bird was handled differently and processed independently. Each taste is preserved, allowing the consumer to get the most out of the scent and flavours.

Zameen doz (Awadhi) : In Urdu, the phrase Zameen doz translates to Inside Earth. Traveling hunters and nomads traditionally produced this fish meal, which is cooked by burying it under the ground. People have abandoned slower cooking techniques throughout time in favour of this real cooking approach, oblivious to the fact that we are not only destroying our own Indian cuisine but also failing to pass along the rich heritage of our own cuisine to future generations.

Aktori (Himachal Pradesh) : Aktori is a typical Pahari dish that comes from the Himachal Pradesh region of India. Usually made for celebrations and happy occasions, this delicious treat. It's simple and hassle-free to prepare this delectable dessert. It is prepared by combining buckwheat and wheat flour, which is then pan-fried to resemble a pancake. Enjoy the delicious flavours direct from the mountains by topping the dish with honey and ghee. This recipe is ideal for you if you prefer to offer some variety to your meals by bringing something that is both new and traditional to the table.

Hangover Cure Stew (Haejang-guk) : Hangover cure stew was invented in South Korea in the early 900 CE. It is a type of soup that is traditionally made with beef, vegetables, and a variety of herbs and spices. The soup is said to be effective in treating the symptoms of a hangover, such as headaches, nausea, and fatigue. There are a number of different recipes for hangover cure stew, but the basic ingredients usually remain the same. The soup is typically served hot, and it can be either thick or thin, depending on personal preference. Some people also add a bit of alcohol to the soup, such as bourbon or brandy, which is said to further help with the symptoms of a hangover.

Nettle pudding: dates back to 6000 BCE in Britain and is considered the oldest known recipe in the world. It is a very thick, light mousse-like dessert made from nettles, milk, and eggs. In the 18th century, nettle pudding was a staple of the English diet. It was thought to help with digestion and strengthen the heart. Nettles were also believed to have medicinal properties because they were known to be rich in iron. Nettle pudding has been popular for centuries, although it wasn't until recently that we learned how nutritious it actually is! Nettles are packed with vitamin C, iron, and magnesium—all nutrients that are beneficial for your health.

Lamb Meatballs With Sour Sauce: This mouthwatering dish was penned down by Muhammad bin Hasan al-Baghdadi in the 12th century. He wrote his cookbook called Kitab al-Ṭabīḫ, the Book of Dishes (as far as original titles go) and is found in its authentic state in the library of Istanbul, Turkey. The lamb meatballs are spiced with coriander, pepper, cinnamon, onions and saffron and served with a full-bodied jus. They are typically served with sprigs of mint and pomegranate seeds; a combination that is still amazing and widely used. To be honest, this dish sounds delicious and is quite easy to make.

Grenville Sweet Potato Pudding: England's Grenville family has provided the world with this unusual yet fascinating 'sweet potato pudding' recipe from circa 1640-1750. Although it doesn't technically look like a pudding - it is basically just mashed sweet potato in a tray with cinnamon and sugar and butter, the flavours are delish! Interestingly, there is a version from Jamaica around too, that looks slightly different but uses sweet potatoes as well as their main ingredient. Whichever one you choose, it's definitely worth a try if you've got some forgotten potatoes lingering in your cupboard and are looking for an easy afternoon snack or dessert.

The Rap Cake: is a delicacy that originated in Croatia and is mainly made of dough, almonds and Maraschino liquor. The legacy says that it was first served to Pope Alexander III in 1177 when he blessed the Cathedral in Rab. Rab, by the way, is an island of Croatia and the Rab cake is its signature delicacy, whereas other islands have their own trademark cake. Considering that this country seems to be almost solely made out of islands - with a staggering count of over a 1000 islands, I can only imagine how many cakes there must be around.

www.ingramcontent.com/pod-product-compliance
Ingram Content Group UK Ltd.
Pitfield, Milton Keynes, MK11 3LW, UK
UKHW022021190726
13853UKWH00005B/2050

9 798889 861331